More than Wolverine

More than Wolverine

An Alaska Wilderness Trapline

By Jeremiah Wood

ISBN: 978-0-9998894-3-5

This book is dedicated to Jim Firmin and the trappers of the greater Fort Yukon area, past and present.

Table of Contents

Also by Jeremiah Wood:

Walter Arnold, Maine Trapper: Stories from one of the Last Mountain Men

A Fall Fur Hunt in Maine: An 1859 Trapping Expedition in the North Woods

The Journey Begins

It's five in the morning. Dark and cold. Early February in northern Maine. I'm awake, alive and excited, and I'm pulling out of the driveway. I've been planning for this day for almost a year, and now it's here. It'll be the longest trip I've ever taken to check traps, my destination about three thousand air miles away on a trapline in the Alaska bush.

I look behind me on the back seat of the pickup truck. The big suitcase is there, and beside me on the passenger's seat my backpack remains where I put it earlier. Not sure why I keep double and triple checking for everything. I ought to know I have everything by now. I packed and repacked numerous times, tossing aside excess items that took too much space or were too heavy. I spent months shopping for cold weather gear while trying to minimize the tendency warm clothing has to fill up a luggage bag, and had hammered out a wardrobe I thought was going to work. I still wonder if it actually will.

The drive from remote northern Maine consists of about a hundred miles of winding roads through an endless forest with little else but trees and moose, and the occasional house. After that is about a hundred more miles of the quietest interstate highway in the Northeast. Each trip reminds me why I live up here. Some hate it, but folks like me love it. It's a small taste of remote living and wild places that can make you crave the real thing in a place like Alaska.

Bangor. 08:30. I'm the first person at the bus stop. It's actually the first time I've taken a bus like this before. I don't know much about the procedure, except that missing the bus means missing my flight — a pretty strong incentive to show up early. Tyson Porter dropped me off. He's keeping my truck at his place for the duration of the trip. Tyson's going to college here, in the same fisheries program I graduated from quite a few years ago. Good kid. His older brother Cole and I passed the time talking trapping and dreaming of Alaska quite a lot not too long ago. Kind of surreal that I'm actually going there.

The bus boarding, tickets, luggage, and stops are all pretty simple once you figure it out. Guess I was worried about nothing. We're just about to Boston.

It gets a little crazy at Logan International Airport. Did I mention I'm not too experienced with cities and travel? Makes me nervous, all those people. I think back to the times I traveled across the country in the past. Things are manageable west of the Mississippi, open and mostly quiet. But to get back to the forest of northern Maine, it's one heck of a mess of cities, roads and frustration to get through. Now I'm in the middle of it.

TSA is funny. Sometimes they let you right through. Other times, not so much. My backpack is completely stuffed with items I've decided I'll need for three weeks in the woods. One of the TSA agents is apparently fascinated by this. Not in a good way either. She takes my pack off the conveyer belt and over to a table, and proceeds to take every single item out of it, inspecting each one. Meanwhile I'm in the x-ray machine and getting the old pat down.

The guy is apparently intrigued by the fact that I have two fleece pullovers, one on top of the other. He keeps rubbing the left side of my chest with his gloved hand, looking for God knows what. I make a joke to try and lighten the mood.

"I'm going to Alaska, need all the clothes I can carry" I remark lightly. I get no response, not even a change in facial expression. But finally he lets me through, and I'm back to repacking my gear on an airport bench. The airport is packed. About a month from now, the COVID-19 pandemic that changed the world will have started, but today, it's business as usual. People come and go, occasionally stealing glances at me and my stuff. Finally one polite, middle aged woman has to stop.

"Wow, those are some big boots! What have you got those for? Must be going someplace cold!"

I'm a little annoyed by the attention, but what the heck, I'll play.

"I'm going to Alaska, going to stay in a cabin in the woods and trap for three weeks."

Her eyes become as wide as saucers.

"Boy, I hope you're safe! Stay warm!"

She quickly rejoins the fast flowing crowd making its way back and forth across the terminal. I'm not sure whether she's more confused as to why I'm going there, or scared for me.

Before long I'm on the flight to Seattle. It's a long flight. Six and a half hours long. Longer than any flight I've been on before. When booking it I was pleasantly surprised I could get from Boston to Fairbanks with only one layover, but now I'm paying for it. I'm in a painstakingly crowded middle seat, and the woman on one side of me has a raging cold. Did I mention it was long?

By the time we reach Seattle it seems like the day ought to be over, but we gained three hours crossing time zones, so it's technically still Sunday. And the airport has some pretty good food for a guy on a restricted diet. The nighttime flight isn't terrible, although I've lost all hope of getting any sleep. I've never been able to sleep in vehicles or planes. Plus, I'm kind of getting excited.

I'm sitting next to a high school athlete and her mom, on their return trip from some tournament. I can't even remember the sport. Basketball? No, that wasn't it. Anyway, it's important to them, which is what matters. I think they said they live in North Pole, a town of a couple thousand, outside of Fairbanks. But it could be just about any suburb in America. They think it's interesting that I'm coming to their home state to trap, but don't have any further questions. It's kind of a reminder that no matter where you go, most of society these days doesn't know trapping exists, or that the pursuit of fur is what settled many of these places. That's okay. They're nice people. And we're almost there.

Three o'clock A.M., local time, Fairbanks Alaska, I'm off the plane, across the airport and over to baggage claim. I look around for a few seconds, and I spot Jim. Must be him. It is. After twenty-six hours of travel, I've arrived.

How I Got Here

While we're standing around at baggage claim in the Fairbanks airport, exchanging pleasantries and getting caught up, I think back to how this whole trip began. It started with Trapping Today, a website I started more than a decade ago to share news and information with trappers. I post updates on the fur market and fur prices, share trapping news stories and articles I've written from experiences on my own trapline. It started slow, but the site gained traction sometime over the years, to the point where thousands of trappers check in to read articles each month. Jim was one of those trappers. He'd make the occasional comment on articles from time to time, sharing observations from his Alaska bush trapline. Like I did with most other commenters, I enjoyed the feedback and interaction, but never put a face, or voice, to the name. Just another trapper. Like me.

It's often difficult to communicate thoughts, emotions, tone, perspective and all of those other parts that make up us humans through written word. That's why I started a podcast at the beginning of 2018. I'd been listening to podcasts a fair bit by then. It was amazing how much more effectively podcasters were able to communicate with others through audio than with words. It only makes sense, and isn't really anything new – TV and radio have been effective media for decades for just that reason. But this was different. The new emerging world of podcasting allowed listeners to choose what they wanted to listen to and when. They could take their shows anywhere and digest information and entertainment while driving in the car, turning wrenches at work, sitting on the couch, or even running around in the woods. A podcast appealed to me as a great way to build the Trapping Today audience and community. And it worked. Before long, hundreds of trappers began listening to my weekly podcast episodes. Jim was one of them.

In the Trapping Today podcast, I covered all kinds of topics, from advice to beginners looking to start a trap line to commentary on trapping news stories, to my personal trapping experiences, and many things in between. From the beginning, it was a wildly effective way to connect with folks as a real human being, and soon people from all over the country who I'd never met knew more about me than some of my closest friends! It was pretty cool.

Since before I'd set my first trap as a high school kid in northern Maine, I'd dreamed of someday moving to the Alaska bush, building a cabin, running a trap line and living that remote, wild life. I'd been to a lot of places and experienced great things over the years, but the Alaska dream had never materialized. Now, with a wife, two young kids, a farm and a full-time job, along with this trapping stuff, it had become pretty obvious that the old dream was going to remain just that. It wasn't a terrible reality. I'd pieced together a pretty good living so far, enjoyed what I did, and had very few regrets......except for that Alaska thing. The more I talked about trapping on the podcast, the more those old dreams of a bush trap line emerged in those conversations with the trapping community each week.

I'm a voracious reader with a dangerous tendency to latch onto a topic and go deep down a rabbit hole until I've consumed every bit of information I can on the subject. Trapping in Alaska is a pretty dangerous subject to start on, because there's enough material there to bury a man for years. So early on I became, and remain today, buried in the genre of Alaska wilderness literature. I began sharing summaries, excerpts and pieces of information from these books with listeners to the podcast, and that's where my connection with Jim began.

One week I spent a good portion of my podcast talking about "Hunters of the Northern Forest", published by Richard K. Nelson in 1973. Nelson was an anthropologist studying wilderness survival adaptations of northern cultures. The book describes the hunting, fishing, gathering and trapping techniques of the Alaskan Kutchin (now termed Gwich'in), which Nelson learned during his nine month stay in the remote village of Chalkyitsik, Alaska, well above the Arctic Circle. The book could in some ways be described as a trapping book as much as a study of anthropology. Rumor has it that Nelson became so intrigued by the trapping lifestyle of the villagers that he was criticized in academic circles for focusing too much on trapping in the book. As a fellow trapping enthusiast, I think I know exactly how he felt.

In those days, much like today, there were virtually no jobs for the residents of remote Alaska villages. The market for wild furs, however, was extraordinary. A trapper could often earn the equivalent of a full time living in the Lower 48 by running a successful trap line during the winter months. Beginning in the mid 1800's and up until the modern day downturn in the fur market, Interior Alaska natives had adjusted their lifestyles and entered as participants in the cash economy through the harvest of animal furs. Nelson followed several trappers from Chalkyitsik out to their long trap lines, staying in makeshift shelters and camps for days or weeks at a time as they worked to harvest fur. These were hard working men who provided for their families from the land, lived in an incredibly vast area of beautiful wilderness, and tested their wits against wild animals every day. They were men I'd dreamed of being.

I got an email from Jim Firmin shortly after my ramblings on "Hunters of the Northern Forest" aired on the podcast. I don't remember all the details, aside from "my trap line is xx miles from Chalkyitsik". Jim was running a modern day trap line in the same country I'd been reading about, and absent mindedly dreaming about. He left a phone number. There was no way I wasn't going to call this guy and learn more.

The first time I called Jim I think we talked for about three hours. We went through about 50 years of his own history, as well as about 50 years of trappers who came before him in the Fort Yukon-Chalkyitsik country. Thankfully for me, this guy was a talker! I did my best to ask questions and soak it up. How did he get there? Find a trap line? What was the country like? How many people still trapped? What was village life like? Could you make a living trapping there? How many cabins? How many miles of trail? What did he do in the summer? I was learning about a world I'd almost chosen myself. It was kind of surreal.

Jim and I started to exchange emails on a regular basis. Like me, he was intrigued by both history and Alaska bush trapping, and he introduced me to a pile of additional books and oral histories of northern trappers that I'd not known of before. As is usually the case, more reading led to more questions, observations, sharing of ideas, and yes, more dreaming. Jim agreed to come on the podcast for an interview. We chatted for about an hour about how he started out trapping as a young man, how he and his brother moved to Fort Yukon with the dream of becoming full time trappers, and what played out over the next 40 years.

At the beginning of the interview, Jim had jokingly suggested I "come on up" to experience his Alaska trap line first hand. A joke, no doubt, I figured. Everybody makes offers like that, not meaning it, and most people accept such offers, not meaning to act on it either. But after our conversation he reiterated. I really was invited to come up and join him on the line. I paused for a moment. And then I thought about it for a few days.

I'd never been on a real vacation before. After graduating high school I'd gone straight to college, from college to grad school, and from grad school to a full time job. In my professional career since then, all of my earned vacation time had been spent either on local hunting, fishing and trapping, or working on the cattle farm my wife and I established in 2013. With limited finances and so many interests close to home, the idea of a long distance vacation had never even entered my mind. Now I had the opportunity to experience one of my lifelong dreams. And opportunities like this don't come along every day.

It was April. I was driving downstate, on that long quiet highway, to pick my wife and two boys up from the airport on their return from Montana, their annual trip to visit her side of the family. I'd been home working and taking care of house and farm, and thinking a lot about a trip to Alaska. In between catching up on events during the three hour ride home, I played my most recent podcast episode in the car. I'll admit I did it for selfish reasons. My wife's always been a supporter of me and my pursuits, and I wanted to give her a more thorough understanding of this Alaska trapping dream I'd talked about in the past. So we listened to Jim talk about his trap line, the area, its rich history, and our shared ideas about the lifestyle he lived. And then, I presented my proposal for a three week trip to trap in Alaska. The answer was yes.

It was time to prepare. With the family on board and approval from work, I had about ten months to save the money and gather the gear I needed for the trip. I immediately began to understand why normal people plan vacations. I can honestly say that every single day in that ten month period, I anticipated the trip. I'd wake up each morning with the thought: "I'm going to Alaska!". When things got tough at work or at home, or I just plain got bored with what I was doing, I'd remember: "I'm going to Alaska!". It was an incredible motivator and morale booster, and reiterated to me the idea that having something to look forward to is a key aspect to happiness in life.

I immediately began saving money. Fortunately the podcast was gaining momentum and I had picked up a few sponsors. The ad dollars went straight into the "Alaska" account I'd set up at the local credit union. Special projects and sales of used traps on Ebay started to add up. It turns out that when you prioritize something and you have plenty of time to save, you can probably put together more money than you think. I wasn't going to have to pay for a place to stay or a guide fee, which was good in more ways than one. I know plenty of folks who pay others for outdoor experiences, but I never have, and I think it would feel quite foreign to me. The greatest expenses of the trip would be airline tickets, the Alaska nonresident trapping license, and cold weather gear.

Jim and I had decided on a two to three week period in early February. I was able to take time off work during that window, the ice conditions would be safe, he would still be running his trap line, the days would be getting longer, and chances for a cold snap bringing -50 degree weather that late in the winter were small. An added bonus was the limited demand for flights to Alaska that time of year, making ticket prices quite reasonable. I found that by taking a bus to Boston I could get a quick, low priced flight to Fairbanks. From there I purchased a flight to Fort Yukon. This 140 mile flight, in a relatively small plane with just a few passengers and mail, would cost nearly half what it cost to go the 3,000+ miles from the East Coast to Fairbanks.

Cold weather gear was the next challenge. Although we do get some cold weather during our northern Maine winters, I knew it was nothing compared to what interior Alaska experiences. I get cold fairly easily, and being cold and miserable wasn't one of the reasons I wanted to do this trip. Jim and I went back and forth by phone, email and text message discussing cold weather gear. Fortunately, he happened to be very close to the same size as I am, meaning I could borrow a few key items it would be difficult to transport - a parka and bunny boots. I pieced together the rest of the outfit - what I had at home and what I purchased at a local L.L. Bean factory outlet and various online shops - over the course of several months. It included lots of warm socks, layers and layers of fleece and polypropylene, several pairs of thermal underwear, wool and fleece pants, a down jacket, arctic mitts, a fur hat, neck warmers, face masks and more. All had to fit in a 50 pound suitcase and a carry-on.

There was another wrinkle in the plans. The past winter had been a life changing one for me, as it marked the end of my decade-long battle with inflammatory back pain. The progressively worsening pain had resulted in a series of doctor visits, chiropractic adjustments, diagnostic tests, X-rays and MRI's. It was eventually determined that I had axial spondyloarthritis. In plain English, that means arthritis of the spine, and is typically used to describe the early stages of ankylosing spondylitis, an autoimmune condition

11

causing the immune system to attack healthy tissues in the sacroiliac joints and lower back, and work its way up the spine.

Long term prognosis for patients with AS isn't good. There is no known cure. Eventually the inflammation and calcium deposition (think bone spurs) leads to permanent fusion of the vertebrae, meaning I could look forward to being hunched over and crippled, but nobody knew when it would get to that point, as the disease progresses differently among individuals. I was told that the only treatment options were anti-inflammatory drugs to slow the inflammation, and TNF inhibiting drugs that put my immune system in check. That's a great way to stop your immune system from attacking itself, but what about when you need it to attack diseases? Some research suggests increased incidences of cancer and other diseases among patients taking TNF's. These I would have to take for the rest of my life. At age 35, considering the costs and honestly quite terrifying side effects, I wasn't excited about going that route. But the back pain I woke up to each morning was a constant reminder that I needed to do something. I declined any treatment right off and went on a month long journey of internet research and at-home experiments. I tried just about everything – exercise, yoga, tai-chi, fasting, health supplements, 100% organic diet, vegetarian, and so on. And finally, somehow, I stumbled onto the answer that changed everything.

I know it's off topic, but I'll share a couple of resources here in the event they may help you or someone you know with an autoimmune disease. I found the research of Dr. Alan Ebringer, professor of immunology at King's College in London, and a book based on his work written by Carol Sinclair titled "The IBS Low-Starch Diet". Dr. Ebringer's research suggested that placing AS patients on a low starch diet resulted in drastic improvements in their condition. He theorized that AS is the result of an immune system reaction to a specific group of microbes – *klebsiella* – that feed on starch in the large intestine. Thus, a reduction in starch intake resulted in lower levels of these bacteria, and a lessened autoimmune reaction.

My wife and I kept track of my back pain level each morning. All of the diet and exercise I'd done for a month resulted in little to no improvement in the pain. After diving deep into the Ebringer theory I decided to go completely starch free for a week to see what would happen. Now that's not as easy as it might sound. When you look at it in detail, it's almost impossible to find food at the grocery store these days that doesn't contain starch. Pasta, grains, cereal, bread, cookies, battered foods, potatoes, carrots, bananas…..the list goes on. Even the vast majority of salad dressings and sauces have starch in them to achieve the proper thickness. It was a challenge just to piece together a week long menu that didn't contain starch. Meats, dairy, green vegetables, nuts and berries were about it.

I went completely starch free for a week, and magic happened. My back pain started improving after the first couple of days, and at the end of the week, it was at half the normal level. Now, instead of getting out of bed with a 5-7 of 10 on the pain scale, I was at a 3. So I kept going. My wife and I couldn't believe it. Part of us thought it was a fluke. So one night I ate a healthy serving of mashed potatoes with dinner. The pain began again after a few hours, and the next morning it was pain level 7. After two more days starch free, it subsided. I'm still beside myself just thinking about it, and if it hadn't happened directly to me, I probably wouldn't believe it. But by completely removing starch from my diet, I was able to eliminate inflammatory back pain and avoid the long, dreadful path of a debilitating disease. I can't imagine being more fortunate.

So at this point, I'd been starch free for months, and my back pain was gone. Pain level zero. The few times we tried to test out a food item, like carrots or quinoa, the pain returned with a vengeance. So we knew we were on the right path with the diet. But that meant restaurants, fast food, and long trips were a huge challenge, and a couple weeks in the Alaska bush, where mac and cheese and pilot bread are major staples, was starting to intimidate me.

My wife and I came up with a list of all the starch free food options we could think of, factored in size and shelf life, and got to work. We began to fill USPS Priority Mail Large Flat Rate boxes with dry foods – almonds, pistachios, dried fruit, dark chocolate, trail mix, pumpkin and sunflower seeds, cheese crisps, pepperoni, bacon bits, and grain free granola.

We blanched, vacuum sealed and froze packs of kale and spinach from the garden. We picked apples and peeled, dehydrated and vacuum sealed them. I slaughtered a beef steer on the farm and made beef jerky, summer sausage and snack sticks with much of the meat, and vacuum sealed and froze it.

In all, we shipped five boxes to Jim's home, more than 3,000 miles away, for about a hundred bucks. Since the temperature rarely exceeds the freezing level there after October, he had plenty of freezer space and the semi-perishables would keep. And now I wouldn't have to worry about choosing between hunger and back pain. Sometimes obstacles that seem insurmountable don't turn out to be that bad, given a little time and effort to figure things out.

From Fairbanks

The food's here, Jim's here, I'm here, and now we're just waiting with the crowd at baggage claim in hopes my clothing made the trip from Maine on time. We're flying to the bush tomorrow, so it's kind of an important detail. There it is - it looks like Alaska Airlines came through. I pick up the heavy bag as it tries to race by me on the conveyer, a little unsteady after the long sleepless journey. I don't think anyone really notices. It's 3 A.M., after all.

I snap out of my grogginess just as soon as we step outside the airport doors. It's about 20 below zero. Sure, I've experienced it this cold many times before in northern Maine, but not in travel clothes. It's cold! We pass by other vehicles as we shuffle out to Jim's car. Most have a light skiff of snow on them. Many are plugged in to the electrical outlets that line the edge of the parking lot. It strikes me as a nice feature, not to have to cold start your vehicle after returning home from a long journey.

We drive through parts of Fairbanks in the dark. It's all new to me, but what strikes me the most is the shape of the trees. Big, towering spruce trees loom just about everywhere there isn't a building, lawn or parking lot. I'm pretty sure these are white spruce, also common back home, but their shape is altogether different here. The traditional triangular shape with wide, sweeping branches at the base tapering to a point at the top doesn't exist here. These trees are shaped more like cylinders - narrow bases and wide tops - with little taper. It's an interesting difference in morphology that I somehow didn't pick up on while watching dozens of hours of Alaska shows on TV. I imagine there's some sort of scientific explanation for it. I read somewhere that the cylindrical shape helps the trees shed snow so their branches don't break. But our triangle trees in northern Maine see a lot more snow than the spruces do here.

We drive by the Alaska Raw Fur Company. It's a nice looking building, with what looks like a beautiful showroom inside. But it's 3:30 AM, so we don't take the tour. Joe and Sandy Mattie have run this wild fur business since 1979, and along with another Fairbanks buyer, Joe probably handles most of the fur that comes out of trap lines in the Interior. Fur buyers like Mattie play a critical role in the lives of Alaska trappers. Those who run long trap lines and rely on fur for an important chunk of their annual income tend to build a close relationship with their buyer. For many years Joe, a pilot and a trapper himself, would fly to the remote villages to bid on collections of fur and visit trappers in outlying cabins to buy their fur and often deliver much needed supplies.

We get to Jim's Fairbanks house, not to be confused with his Fort Yukon house. Though they lived in Fort Yukon for decades, Jim and his wife Susan, a Gwich'in Athabaskan woman from the village, split their time between the two places now. Their children are grown and now they have have grandkids, one of the big draws of town. Then there are groceries, supplies, hospitals, and all of the modern day conveniences most Americans enjoy. There's a disadvantage to having multiple homes and multiple cars though. It stretches the budget. So nothing is fancy, but all is functional.

We pour in out of the cold with gear and luggage and sit down at the kitchen table to chat a bit. Then he shows me the facilities and the futon in the guest bedroom. I'm still wired. It's hard to fall asleep.

It's 5:30 and the coffee's on. We have to be at Wright's Air Service for 9, since the plane to Fort Yukon leaves at 10. That leaves a couple of hours to talk trapping at the kitchen table. By the time Susan's up, Jim and I have maps spread out all over the table and I'm learning who trapped where, the location of old cabins, land status, modern day lines, and just about everything else.

I think Susan's pretty amused while she makes us breakfast. She probably figures Jim's finally found someone who's willing to talk trapping for as long as he is, and I'm there soaking up every word. Soaking is probably a poor description, because my short term memory is terrible. If I don't write down names or hear them a dozen times in short order they're forgotten. Other small details suffer the same fate. But writing in a notebook during coffee time at the kitchen table on the first day would probably be considered poor form, so I try to be a sponge.

We arrive at Wright's just as I'm beginning to take in Fairbanks in the daytime. The air service terminal is a nice little building, across the airfield from Fairbanks International Airport, and surrounded by small private hangars, specialty flying services, and a smattering of bush planes tied down alongside the runway. Wright is one of the only remaining companies that service the small villages of the interior. Many have started, struggled and failed in the mail, freight and passenger service business in rural Alaska. For this flight, they're the only game in town.

Even though I'm new to this bush flying thing, it seems pretty simple. Show your ticket (I'd purchased mine a month ago), weigh your bags, pay for the excess weight ($1.40/lb) and sit down and relax in a chair in the lobby with the other soon-to-be passengers. Most of the people look like they do this regularly. There's a group of young guys who look military, maybe civil service. Sounds like they're going to a village for a work project. The woman sitting across from me is talking on her phone about education in remote villages – must work for the school system.

Jim and I walk out to the entryway of the main building. We're a bit overdressed and it's cooler out there. A couple of older native men are out there talking, but not in English. I assume they're speaking Gwich'in. Jim knows them – one used to trap. He says hello. His name is Henry Flet. He's just flown into town for a doctor's appointment and is waiting for a ride. They make a little small talk about fur prices and Henry's family's old trap line. I recognize the name from a 1940's paper I'd read describing the economic impact of trapping in the Fort Yukon area. His grandfather Jacob had the trap line at the time with Henry's father, Solomon. Henry grew up there, in the bush. He laments a bit about how nobody spends time in the bush these days, everyone stays in town. He no longer traps. "Too old" he says.

The plane's ready. We line up, get the go-ahead, and walk out and start piling in. I'm not a plane guy, so I can't describe it much except to say it's a prop plane that would probably max out at 15 or 20 passengers. There are a dozen of us, our gear, and a bunch of mail. The pilot wastes no time ensuring we're situated, going through his checks, and getting on down the runway. Jim tells me he's a Newman, from the Yukon River village of Beaver. No doubt he's descended from Turak Newman, legendary Inupiak Eskimo from the Arctic Slope and gold miner and freighter in the Chandalar

District. Beaver is an interesting place – a village of Eskimo descendents in the middle of Athabaskan country. Their history is a unique one, dating back to the early 1900's, when Japanese trader and gold prospector Frank Yasuda helped lead a group of starving Eskimos south from Barrow, over the Brooks Range and to the Yukon River where they established Beaver, still going strong today at a population of 84 as of the last census. The village is a ways downstream of Fort Yukon. We won't see it on this trip.

We climb up out of Fairbanks, and for the next hour I'm glued to the window of the plane, taking as much of it in as I can. City streets and suburbs almost immediately give way to large patches of timber, interspersed with a few roads, a subdivision here, a dog mushing trail there, a couple of large gold mines, and finally, just about nothing.

It isn't long before everything I look down on is wilderness – streams, rivers, lakes, trees, and what I assume is tundra. It gives a whole new meaning to the word 'vast'.

Fairbanks from the air

I imagine cutting trail, establishing a remote trap line through parts of the forest we pass. Large patches of burned ground is littered with downed timber from recent forest fires. In green, well forested areas, many of the spruce trees appear to have bent, or curled tops, leaning one way or the other. I can't decipher whether there's some sort of phenomenon associated with that, or if that's just the way they grow. It all looks so wild – tough country to even cut trails through, let alone tame, if one had the inclination.

Entering the Flats

We have one stop before reaching Fort Yukon: Birch Creek. We make our way towards it as Beaver Creek winds its way in and out of view below. It looks like a pretty amazing place for a trapline, with a beautiful spruce forest lining the banks and numerous backwater sloughs and lakes. But distinct patches of dark blue that signify open water add a bit of a reality check. You'd need to know that country and its hazards well before venturing on the creek, and even then it could be dangerous. I see no trails, no cabins, no smoke.

We circle the village of Birch Creek and touch down on the runway. It's a nice runway, and I'm surprised how large it is given the size of the grouping of houses it serves. If not for the runway, I realize, there wouldn't be a town here. Jim tells me the population is around twenty souls. No school. As the plane stops, two men pull up on snowmobiles (they call them 'snowmachines' out here), one to pick up Isaac James – the man I heard talking with Henry Flet at the Airport. James is a small man with big boots and heavy gear. In the few short moments I've seen him, he strikes me as a proud, quiet man who doesn't worry about small details. I assume he's like a lot of people from small villages who often become larger-than-life characters compared to their city dwelling counterparts. Considering we have a few like that in small town northern Maine, Alaska must be off the charts.

The other snowmachine carries a young native man and an empty tote sled. Looks like he's here to pick up the village mail. He looks under-dressed for minus twenty degrees. He wears a black baseball cap with symbols and pins on it, and large bold letters, reading "Native Pride".

Passengers and freight are offloaded, and we're back in the air. I notice a snowmachine trail leaving the village, headed toward Fort Yukon. It's not a heavily traveled trail, but shows a fresh track or two. It's the only sign of human activity outside of the huddled group of cabins and the lonely air strip. In the old days, a network of trails like this one connected most of the villages with each other.

With the convenience of air travel, very few of the old trails still exist.

Patterns in the trees

We've entered the Yukon Flats. From the air, it's a fascinating display of river morphology and ecological succession. The active channels of the streams meander through their valleys, their dimensions and angle of each bend seemingly random, but entirely predictable, given valley slope, substrate, precipitation and other variables. I know just enough about fluvial geomorphology to be dangerous, and to realize that for the first time I'm witnessing streams that have been allowed to exist in their natural state for thousands of years without human disturbance. So this is what it looks like. Looking a little more carefully through the window of the plane, I can see where streams have been before. The patterns are evident in the trees – patterns of curves and bends formed by trees of the same age and height, paralleling the active channel, and similar patterns of shorter, younger trees and taller, older trees paralleling the other patterns. They're abandoned stream banks, no longer needed when the channel migrates to a different part of the valley. The stream channels that are abandoned start off as oxbow lakes. Their creation is simple and abrupt. Perhaps a tree falls in just the right place and redirects flow during high water. Perhaps water spills over its bank on an outside bend and carves out a low spot. The low spot grows and grows with more water and erosion, and as it grows it attracts more water in its channel. The stream takes a shortcut, and its former bend is abandoned. These cut-off channels still hold water, but are no longer part of the stream. They are lakes. Bushes grow in around them, and eventually trees. Without the energy of flowing water to transport the silt above them downstream, they begin to fill. Vegetation creeps in. They become meadows.

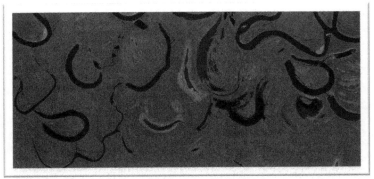

Aerial image of oxbow lakes

We're flying over hundreds of these oxbow lakes in all stages of succession. The Flats are full of them. Some are probably deep enough to hold fish and support healthy populations of muskrats.

23

Most are shallow marshes filled with mud and aquatic vegetation, only navigable in winter when everything's frozen. The collection of them supports a substantial portion of the nesting habitat for North America's waterfowl. Few of these lakes have seen a human being in decades.

The winding streams and slough lakes suddenly give way to a vast expanse of white. I'm looking down at the frozen, snow-covered Yukon River. I expected it would look big, but scale is hard to imagine from a TV screen or Google Earth. The Yukon is more than two miles wide, sprinkled with large islands and various small channels. I notice open water near shore on a few. The white expanse of the lower Porcupine River is just ahead of us, and the roads and houses of a large river village appear below.

The Yukon River and village of Fort Yukon from the air

Fort Yukon

Fort Yukon might be the most storied town in Alaska. If you're a trapper, it certainly is. Alexander Murray established a trading post here for the Hudson's Bay Company in 1847. The Bay was a Canadian company that established outposts in the far north to trade in valuable furs. Alaska was owned by Russia at the time, and an international treaty strictly prohibited the Canadians from conducting business in the territory. Either Murray didn't know he wasn't in Canada, or he didn't care. Either way, the company conducted trade at the junction of the Porcupine and Yukon rivers for the next twenty years, until the United States purchased Alaska from Russia and the military showed up with a U.S. flag and gave the company its walking papers.

The area surrounding Fort Yukon was recognized early on as an incredibly productive and rich country for furbearers. It was inhabited at the time by the Gwich'in people, a group of Athabaskan natives who lived a nomadic lifestyle on the Yukon Flats and surrounding river drainages. The Gwich'in migrated throughout the year in search of caribou, moose, bears and fish. They lived in tents, or makeshift houses constructed from caribou

25

hides, had few worldly possessions, and virtually all of their activities were focused around the search for food. In the book "Shandaa: In My Lifetime", Belle Herbert told stories of the old lifestyle led by natives up and down the Porcupine River, and how difficult it was. Belle was estimated to be close to 120 years old in 1980 when she shared her wisdom from the village of Chalkyitsik.

Harvesting furbearers, though important, played a relatively small role in Gwich'in activities before the arrival of trading posts. The potential to trade animal skins for valuable items such as firearms, ammunition, clothing and food staples brought on a complete lifestyle change for the people. Trapping became an important source of income and allowed for a better standard of living. As a result, it became a pivotal part of the lives of the Gwich'in people and ushered in the transition, for better or worse, to a modern lifestyle. They were now trappers.

In the 100 years following the establishment of the original Hudson's Bay post in 1847, Fort Yukon underwent a gradual transition from being a trading center visited by nomadic family groups to a year-round permanent residence for essentially everyone in the area. Stores, school, hospital, post office, military installation, air travel, and a government welfare system all contributed to the shift. And a gold rush influx, several disease epidemics and a massive flood shaped the town as well. But all the while, the country surrounding Fort Yukon continued to be rich in valuable furbearers, and supported a fur economy that was the area's most important source of income and wealth for quite some time.

The gold rush brought many from the Lower 48 to the Fort Yukon area, but it was the fur resource and the love of the country that kept them there. In 1910, seventeen year old James A. Carroll left his home in Minnesota to join his brother in search of Alaska gold. After a short stint cooking in the Yukon gold camps further upstream, Carroll floated down the river to Fort Yukon, intent on becoming a fur trapper. He partnered up with an old timer that first fall and journeyed forty miles up the Porcupine River, and another 45 or so up the Salmon (now called the Sheenjek) River. They built a cabin and Jimmy, over time, learned to trap. In "Above the Arctic Circle", Carroll tells of his first ten years out in the Alaska bush and shares tales of fellow Fort Yukon fur harvesters.

It wasn't just Carroll either. During the first half of the twentieth century, Fort Yukon was a boom town for fur trappers. They left town in late summer or early fall, in time to make it to their respective trap line cabins, which were scattered about the country. They trapped all winter, with those relatively close by (say, less than 100 miles) often returning for a break at Christmas time. Then it was back to the lines to catch fur until spring, when they floated down the river to town at breakup. Back in Fort Yukon, they'd sell their fur, purchase next year's outfit, swap stories, and yes, party.

Carroll married a local native woman (Fannie Martin), and they eventually had a dozen kids. He settled into town and established a trading post. It's said that about a quarter of the population of Fort Yukon today is comprised of Carroll family members.

We touch down in Fort Yukon and taxi over to the terminal. In addition to us passengers, there's a whole ton of mail to unload. Through some miracle of the U.S. Postal Service (I believe they call it 'bypass mail'), people here can get everyday items shipped from anywhere in the U.S. for the same cost as I can in Maine. No doubt it requires some serious federal subsidies, but it's also a lifeline that helps keep these remote villages afloat. It won't get here in two days or less, but villagers can get free shipping on almost anything out here through Amazon Prime.

We greet a couple of folks outside of the terminal while waiting for our gear. One is Josh Cadzow, who Jim had told me of when I'd asked earlier whether there were any other trappers left here. Josh is a young man, probably close to my age. He works for the tribe, building subsidized houses, runs a dog team in local races, and chases wolves, and occasionally other furbearers, up the Porcupine. His family cabin is upriver from Jim's trap line. The name sounds familiar. Dan Cadzow was an independent trader from New York who built a beautiful home and store at Rampart House, where the river crosses the International Boundary more than 200 miles upstream from here. A small community developed at the site, where Cadzow stayed between 1904 and his death in 1929. It was abandoned shortly after. Josh is taking the plane on its next leg to Chalkyitsik, seemingly just for the heck of it. It's a nice day for a ride.

Jim is walking to his house, just a couple blocks away, to get his vehicle so we can haul all of our stuff over. I'm staying here to keep an eye on the gear. He has to reinstall the battery, which is in the house to keep warm, so it might take a while. I wander inside the terminal and have a look around. A young man is engaged in small talk with the jack-of-all-trades who runs the place. He's looking for a humidifier that was supposed to arrive a week ago, checking to see if it's in on this load. His wife and newly arrived child are kind of anxious to get it. I'm guessing it's work that brought him here — he probably teaches at the school, or maybe works at the health center. Seems like a nice guy.

The young man leaves, and I walk over to the man behind the counter.

"You're from Maine, huh?" I ask him. I've kind of cheated, because Jim already told me about him, but the distinct coastal

28

Maine accent would give him away anywhere. "That's where I came here from".

"Yeah, born and raised in Maine" he says. "You've come a long way. What are you doing here?"

"Trapping".

"Oh, you're with Jim! Okay."

We dive into a conversation. His name is David Bridges, and he moved here more than thirty years ago, a fresh graduate from the University of Maine, to work as a school teacher in Chalkyitsik. He's retired from teaching and runs the terminal these days. He's dressed in heavy Carhartt overalls, big boots and a thick coat, along with the most beautiful hat I've ever seen, made entirely of marten fur. His wife, a native from the village, sewed it by hand.

Bridges has only returned to Maine once, a few years ago, when his mother died. I ask him what it's like to live here. Again I'm fascinated, and intensely curious. I imagine if I'd taken the same leap out of college like I'd been tempted to.

"I love it here. The weather isn't as bad as people think. The summers are great. Brilliant. The bugs aren't that bad. You're from Maine, the bugs aren't any worse than in Maine. It's sunny most of the time. The winters are cold, but not windy. The people are nice."

I'm struck by Bridges' comment about the people because I've heard so many conflicting opinions about the place. The first time I asked someone about Fort Yukon, many years ago, I was told "You don't want to go there. They don't like outsiders and you won't be welcome."

True, this once-booming fur town filled with white trappers and Gwich'in natives living in relative harmony seemed a very welcoming place in James Carroll's day. Today the trappers are gone, and more than 85% of the 500-600 residents who call the village home identify as Native American. I'm guessing that many

29

of the 10% who identify as Caucasian, according to Census Bureau statistics, are here for work, perhaps not permanent fixtures of the local community. I've never spent much time in a place where I was a minority. It strikes me as a bit intimidating.

I think back to a chapter in John Hildebrand's book "Reading The River", where the author stops in Fort Yukon on his long river canoe trip and visits with some of the locals. Either the village was welcoming with open arms, or outsiders would never be accepted in the community, depending who you talked to.

I ask David Bridges about internet availability and other modern conveniences in the town. He speaks of recent improvements, but also offers some hesitation when I mention the potential to attract new residents in.

"We want to discourage that" he says. "They talked about building a road to here too. The problem with a road is, you attract the 'end of the road' types." The irony of these words coming from a Mainer isn't lost on me, but I get it. When you become part of a place, it becomes part of you, and you want to preserve it that way.

Jim finally arrives with the car. It's a Chevy Blazer actually, with door locks, handles and electric windows on the fritz. But it doesn't have to go far. The town only has a few miles of road. He takes me on a tour, first stopping to get water at the town pump. His house has running water, but it'll be a while before the house warms up enough so we can use it. We drive down to the river where parked aluminum boats sit in the snow, as if patiently waiting for spring. There's a barge there too, perhaps past its glory days and facing stiff competition from low cost airfare, but come spring it might just resume hauling cars and other large freight from Circle City.

We drive by the town liquor store, a source of revenue, a source of joy, or a source of pain, and perhaps all three, depending who you ask. Alcoholism is rampant among Alaska native villages.

Whether it's genetic, cultural or otherwise, natives and alcohol don't mix. Many villages have completely banned the sale, importation or possession of alcohol in attempts to stem widespread domestic violence, child neglect, criminal activity, suicide and other problems, with limited success. Some, like Fort Yukon, have decided to allow controlled alcohol sales and use the proceeds to pay for community programs and policing. It's a complicated, emotional issue, and I fail to fully understand it.

We drive past the house of the most famous man in Fort Yukon, United States Congressman Don Young. It's a humble place by Washington standards, but for here, it's pretty nice. Like other dreamers before him, Young moved to Alaska in search of the adventure, lifestyle and opportunity only this place could offer. He tried his hand at commercial fishing, trapping and gold prospecting before working as a school teacher in Fort Yukon. Young won his seat in Congress, Alaska's only House seat, by special election in 1973. Today he's the longest serving member in that institution. Highly opinionated, unwavering in his convictions, and seemingly lacking any filter, I can't imagine anyone fighting for Alaskans as fiercely as Don Young. I don't think he spends much time here anymore, though.

We continue on and see more of the town. Lots of log cabins, their yards littered with freshly cut firewood, snowmachines, and often a few sled dogs. There's the local fuel supplier – the only game in town if you need heating oil. Then there are the government buildings. I'm confused a bit by government structure here. There is the city government, with a mayor, council, manager, police force, etc., and then there is tribal government, which seems to possess many of the same powers. Or maybe not. I don't see a Fish and Wildlife Service office, though I believe the Service has a small presence here, being in the heart of the Yukon Flats National

Wildlife Refuge. There's an Alaska Fish and Game building, but no active office. A seasonal operation, I guess.

I'm reminded of the words of Sam White in Jim Rearden's book "Sam O. White, Alaskan" describing his arrival as a game warden in Fort Yukon: "*I arrived in Fort Yukon at the beginning of winter 1927, the first resident federal Fish and Wildlife agent for the area. This struck many of the old timers as rather funny. The need of regulatory laws for game and fur wasn't apparent to them.*"

Now personally, I'm a big supporter of law and order, and see it as necessary, in most cases, for fish and wildlife conservation. But then there's that part of me, that wild, freedom seeking individualist, who dreams of places so open, free and unpopulated that they don't need much in the way of regulation.

We've seen about all there is to see, and it's close to dark, so we head back. We drive by a young man walking down the street, dressed in far less clothing I'd be comfortable in at this temperature. I wave, but he doesn't wave back. He looks down and continues walking.

We're back at Jim's house. For such a remote village, there sure is a lot crammed into a small area. Houses surround us. You wouldn't know it by the clock, but the day is almost over. A woman walks by with a beautiful fur coat, undoubtedly she's warm. Probably going to get the mail. Another walks past, pleasant and cheery. She says hi to Jim. She's the daughter of Fred Thomas, he tells me. Fred was a legendary trapper who passed away recently at damn near a century old, and he trapped almost up to the very end. He was a trapping mentor to Jim, someone he could bring a question or problem to and receive a well thought out reply. A good guy. I wish I'd met him. A couple of young guys zip by on a snowmobile with a sled and chainsaw in tow. They're heading out to cut firewood. It'll be dark in half an hour.

Up the Porcupine

We're up early, but we don't need to be. It won't be light for at least a couple hours yet. Breakfast, coffee and trapping talk start the day. Now comes the task of assembling the right mix of cold weather clothing. I've thought about this about a thousand times over the past year, but didn't have the minus twenty degree weather, or the full complement of gear, for a test run. I pull clothing out of my suitcase and backpack and lay the items in small piles on the floor. We're headed on a 45 mile snowmachine ride with no place to get warm between town and the cabin. It'll be pretty important to start out with plenty of clothing.

I'm wearing more layers than I'd thought humanly possible. Three pairs of wool socks cover my feet, which are inside a pair of extreme cold weather pac boots. I have three pairs of long underwear on, including a merino wool base layer. A pair of fleece pants inside of a pair of wool pants cover these. Jim lends me a pair of Refrigiwear snow bibs to top it off. My torso is covered by about five or six layers of wool, fleece, and poly blend. I have thick down jacket and a waterproof shell over this. Though I tend to get cold easy, cold doesn't seem possible with all of this stuff on. My head is covered with a thick balaclava and a Mad Bomber rabbit fur hat. I've been told that in native cultures it's often the women who wear rabbit, but it was the warmest hat I could find at a reasonable price, so it'll have to do. Back home I'd be wearing a snowmobile helmet for rides like this, but folks here don't use them, and getting one here from Maine was out of the question. I have a pair of ski goggles that I hope will help block the wind. My hands tend to get cold easy, but with heated handlebars on the snowmachine it shouldn't be a problem during the ride. I have a thin pair of fingerless gloves, some fleece/deerskin mitts, and a pair of big, bulky military surplus mitts to cover these. A box of hand warmers is coming with us too, just in case.

The final piece of the clothing puzzle is the most critical. Jim hands me a parka from his collection. It's a very large, tall jacket with a heavy duty canvas-like outer layer and some insulation. But the most critical part of the parka is the hood, with its fur-lined ruff. The ruff on this one is from either a coyote or a wolf. The coat zips up and out to form sort of a tunnel, closing much of the outside world from most of the wearer's field of vision. As I'm about to experience firsthand, it's a necessary design to block the chilling wind.

It's starting to get light and we're pretty well bundled up, so we make our way outside and begin to assemble the load. Last night we got a good start on trip preparation, taking the two snowmachines out of storage, starting and fueling them up, and beginning to load gear. Each machine will tow a toboggan carrying all of the clothing, food, fuel and other supplies we'll need. I've spent some time examining these toboggans. I haven't seen anything like them elsewhere in my travels, and the same design seems to be universal throughout the village.

Archdeacon of the Yukon, Hudson Stuck, learned the importance of the toboggan about a century ago. In his 1914 book "Ten Thousand Miles with a Dog Sled", Stuck described his team's difficulty in traveling the Yukon Flats with a traditional sled: *"There is little travel on the Flats in winter, and a snow-storm accompanied by wind may obliterate what trail there is in an hour. The vehicle used in the Flats is not a sled but a toboggan, and our first mistake was in not conforming to local usage in this respect. There is always a very good reason for local usage about snow vehicles."*

In addition to being a missionary, priest and adventurer – he organized the first party to reach the summit of Mount McKinley (now known as Denali) - Stuck was a strong advocate for native people across Alaska. By his request, he was buried in the native cemetery in Fort Yukon.

The toboggans we're using are long and narrow with a smooth, flat bottom. No skis protrude from them, although some subtle runners may line the bottom near the outside edges. Their design maximizes the amount of surface area touching the snow, allowing them to float on top of it while other sleds may tend to dig in, plow through and push snow. The bottoms of Jim's toboggans are made of large pieces of smooth teflon material that bend upward at the front. The sides are made of plywood, and holes are drilled every few inches along the top edges of the plywood to accommodate a network of loops created by the weaving and knotting of rope. Each loop serves as a tie-down point to secure cargo or the sled's cover. The cover can be a blanket, a tarp, or as in our case, old canvas material recycled from construction projects. The plywood back of the sled supports a teflon handle, and the sled bottom and two by four framing extends about a foot behind the back, all to accommodate a standing rider.

Traditional toboggan on a narrow trail

Their light weight, narrow design (maybe 16" wide), and large surface area make these toboggans ideal for this country. They can weave through narrow bush trails and around obstacles and float over soft snow, all while hauling a surprising amount of freight. The only thing I don't like is the lack of a fixed hitch. When towed by a rope they like to wander around, and often slam into the back of the machine when you hit the brakes. I wonder if this feature, or lack thereof, is a carryover from the days before snowmachines when these toboggans were hauled by dogs.

Finishing loading doesn't take too long. The greatest portion of our freight is gasoline. We'll be burning a lot of it with the snowmachines and they don't sell it out in the bush. Every ounce used on the trap line has to be hauled in. Gas is more than $6 a gallon in Fort Yukon. We have a large plastic drum full of it and several smaller containers. Food, clothing, survival gear and some trapping supplies fill out the load. We'll be checking traps along the way.

We pull out of the Firmin driveway onto the hard packed snow-covered street a little after 9:30 AM. Jim is driving his newer machine, a Skidoo Tundra, and I'm on his Arctic Cat Bearcat. Each has a wooden cargo box mounted on the rear rack and a toboggan in tow. The sun is up above the horizon and it's warmed to about ten below. Here we go.

Town is quiet this morning as we pass through, with little moving except the smoke rolling out of most every chimney. It doesn't take long to reach the outskirts, and we're on a plowed road with the occasional driveway leading to a home. There's some sort of subdivision of lots outside of town, but most are vacant lots or in some stage of development. I'm on high alert, trying to focus on each turn we take in the event I need to make my way back to town alone. But after a while, it's a little much to keep straight. We're quite a ways out of town now, but the road is still plowed, and suddenly I see a bridge ahead. It's a nice one, too. Probably cost at least half a million to build, from the looks of it. Later I'll learn that the bridge crosses the Sucker River, and that the road and bridge are there to provide access to firewood on tribal lands. Locals call it the 'wood road'.

It's the beginning of our journey and I'm already starting to get cold, though I'm not sure I'd admit it. Jim stops his machine to check on me and the sleds and walks up to me. "You cold?" he asks, knowingly. "Your parka's not zipped all the way up". I've got the parka zipped to my neck, negating the 'tunnel' effect and the protective properties of the ruff. With some added effort, I get the thing zipped up to nose level, and then out, and much of the surroundings disappear from view. My entire field of vision has been reduced to a palm sized opening about six inches in front of my nose. But almost instantly, I'm warm.

We continue down the wood road, which has transitioned to a smaller, narrower, but well packed winding trail. Jim's making good time and I'm going a bit slower with the lack of peripheral vision and the need to turn my body nearly 180 degrees to take the occasional peek at the toboggan behind me. The next turn I make to look back catches me by surprise. There's a man on a snowmachine coming around me. I stop, and he does too. He's a native man, probably about middle age.

"Your toboggan is on its side" he says, pointing behind me. I look back and there it is, tipped over in the trail. "Oh! Wow!" I say. "Has it been that way for a while?"

"Yes" he says, "Just wanted to let you know".

"Thank you".

"Who are you?" he asks, seeming surprised there would be someone out here he didn't know.

"I'm with Jim Firmin, heading up the river".

"Oh, okay. He up ahead?"

I nod, and he takes off up the trail, a big empty sled in tow. I tip the toboggan back up where it belongs. The tall gas container is giving the load a pretty high center of gravity. It'll need some adjustment, but first I'll catch up with Jim. The two machines are on a little lake where the trail forks. The other machine heads off as I pull up to Jim's. He tells me the man who stopped me is Gerald James, out cutting firewood. James is a local jack of all trades and entrepreneur. He runs the barge from Circle to Fort Yukon each summer, does maintenance work, and is an accomplished wolf hunter.

We adjust the load and move on. The trail gets narrower and windier. At some point it breaks out into the frozen, snow-covered water of Eight Mile Slough, which is a side channel to a side channel of the Porcupine River. Ours are now the only fresh tracks in the snow, and the formerly bumpy trail ride gives way to smooth sailing. The slough is a narrow channel with steep, tall sand and gravel banks lined with trees. The sun is just high enough to poke over the tallest spruces and shine rays of light on portions of the channel. We round a corner and spook up a moose, steam rising from its back. It runs in front of the machines for a while before scrambling up the bank and into the trees.

Ice gives way to open water in small portions of the slough, mainly at pinch points where the channel narrows or becomes shallower and the current flows swiftly. We pass on safe ice close by. Jim seems to know where all of these are, and I'm careful to follow his tracks closely. I wonder what would happen if one didn't know how to properly navigate places like this. It's not a place I'd want to travel in the dark.

We break out to a large river channel, but not large enough to be the Porcupine, I think. Turns out it's half the Porcupine. The river is split into two channels here. We're near the mouth of the

Black River, and the trail to Chalkyitsik. It's easy to get turned around in this country, riddled with channels that snake their way through the wide valley, often with no apparent hint as to the direction they plan to go. They connect to and disconnect from various backwater sloughs and lakes in a pattern that changes a little bit with each spring flood.

Jim pulls up to a spot along a high bank on the river and turns off his machine, and it looks like I'll be checking my first set of traps since the long journey from Maine. We walk up the bank through the snow, a fresh few inches of which fell since Jim was last here, and look at a few empty lynx snares. Coming from a place where both lynx trapping and using snares are illegal, this is a new game to me, and I have a lot to learn. But I'm immediately struck by how simple it actually is.

Lynx are constantly wandering through the willow thickets along river banks in search of their primary prey, snowshoe hares, which feed on willows and use them and the surrounding spruces for cover and protection from predators. At this location, Jim's sets are almost too simple to be true. He walks back and forth through the snow a few times to pack down a trail. In the same manner, he makes a couple of side trails off this main trail. Each trail is then guarded with a lynx snare and a few guide sticks. This set works off of a simple concept. A packed trail is easier walking than deep snow, even for a lynx, so they tend to use one when they encounter it. As such, most rabbit-hunting lynx that cross a trail like this will follow it, and (hopefully for the trapper) walk right into the snare.

A trail snare for lynx

Lynx snaring, like most snaring, is an art, and the possibilities for snare style and design are almost endless. The snare of choice on this trap line consists of 1/16" 1x19 galvanized aircraft cable with a wedge lock and a kill spring, with a length of #9 soft wire built in to anchor and support the loop. The loop measures about 8-9" in diameter, a little wider than it is tall, and is set at a height of about 10" from the snow to the bottom of the snare loop. It's painted white to blend in. Throughout North America there are probably as many variations to this setup as there are trappers who hang cable, but this seems to work pretty well for Jim. As a bonus to lynx, it takes wolverine quite effectively as well.

We pack down the fresh snow in the trails, make sure the snares are still functional, and move on. The rest of the journey upriver will be broken up by eight or ten stops to check and maintain traps. When Jim started out in this country more than four decades ago he'd never set a trap before reaching his cabin. Competition was stiff from other trappers and there wasn't a whole lot of fur to catch along the way. And even though the river, being a main highway for public transportation, was pretty much fair game for any trapper, I imagine it would be a bit uncomfortable making sets adjacent to the territory claimed by the old timers. Over the years, as fur prices fell and trappers dropped off, he started setting traps in the abandoned ground along the river corridor. There's more fur here now and almost nobody else is harvesting it, so there's a great opportunity to pick up some extra fur between town and the cabin.

A simple cubby set for lynx and wolverine

42

Crossing the river, we climb the opposite bank and wind the machines through an opening dotted with willows and small spruce trees. At the base of one of the spruces is a set. It's a foothold trap set for wolverine and lynx, with a piece of lynx meat wired to the tree and the trap set at its base, a foot or so back. The bait has been chewed to the bone, and the trap and surrounding area are covered with fox tracks. Snow-blown and frozen to the ground, the trap didn't fire when the fox came in. He got a free meal, and we're out a fox pelt.

A few miles later we pull up to a nondescript flat along the riverbank to our right, and Jim says it looks like there's something in his snare. I jump off the machine and race over to check it out. He says it looks like a fox, maybe.

One of our first lynx

I get closer and it appears to be a lynx, dead and frozen, covered in the fresh snow. My heart leaps. We got one! It's a beautiful animal with thick, full fur. Wow! Jim walks up to where I'm at and speaks up.

"We got another one. Look!" I was so enthralled by the first lynx that I didn't even think of the fact that he probably had more sets here. Up ahead in the trail stands a live lynx, caught in a foothold trap and looking in our direction. Jim gets an extra snare from the snowmachine and attaches it to a pole taken from the surrounding willows. He's going to demonstrate to me how to dispatch a lynx. After I take a couple of pictures, he uses the pole to slip the snare over the animal's head and gives a tug as it tightens around the neck. He lifts the lynx in the air and after a short struggle, it's quiet and calm. From start to finish, it takes probably all of thirty seconds.

There's nothing pretty, nothing glorious about killing animals. It's a necessary evil and a reminder that death is a common part of life out here. Some people think trappers are cruel. I disagree. Watching this lynx die bothers me, just like it would bother anyone who's human. Taking the life of any animal is a serious matter. But what sets hunters and trappers apart is our willingness to take part in this necessary process of death. It brings us closer to the harsh reality of nature and reinforces our role at the top of the food chain, and our responsibility in helping Mother Nature manage these populations of wildlife.

Lynx population numbers fluctuate in decade-long cycles, in direct correlation with the abundance of snowshoe hares. This year is predicted to be the last of the high years, and a population crash is coming soon. That means that the majority of lynx we're catching this year would, if unharvested, have been destined to a long, slow, and yes, cruel, death by starvation as they compete with other lynx for the few remaining hares in these willows. As a general rule I don't think it's appropriate to lend human characteristics to wild animals. It assumes a lot of animals, and perhaps gives humans more credit than we deserve. But for the sake of argument, if I were this lynx, and I knew the future that was to come, thirty seconds at the end of a snare pole would seem quite un-cruel by comparison.

In all the excitement I haven't thought to ask Jim if he had any other sets at this spot. A quick glance further down the trail answers that question. A third lynx is there, dead in a snare. Three lynx in three sets! It's been quite a stop. We remake the sets, load our catch in the sleds and continue upriver.

The river is at its full size now. It's massive, measuring more than a thousand feet across. Other than a few places to watch for open water, travel is easy. Sometime around two or three in the afternoon we take a course for the left bank and a faint trail that leads to a patch of tall timber. The wind has drifted some of the fresh fallen snow into the trail, making the ascent of the steep bank a challenge. We stop and carve out an opening in the vertical drift with a pack shovel that's stored under the seat of the Bearcat I'm driving. After that, it's a breeze. We weave through willows and spruce for a short ways, and I see a cabin in an opening up ahead. So this is it.

The small clearing on this flat above the Porcupine River is lined with towering spruce trees, of a size that can be a little hard to find this far north of the Arctic Circle. The stand extends to the north and west, but to the south is a thicket of younger growth, with trees so tightly packed I wouldn't dare try to walk through them. The clearing has a cabin on each end. One is a tiny old shack that's been here for decades, and the other is so new it doesn't even have a door on it yet. We head into the new cabin and I check out my home for the next two weeks.

The trapline cabin

The one thing all cabins in the winter woods have in common is that it takes an agonizingly long time to get them heated up. Job number one is to get a fire going in the big barrel stove. Jim does this, while I take a look at the recent construction project. Aside from relying on two heavy blankets to shelter us from the elements rather than a proper door, the cabin looks really good. It measures 14x16 feet, with the stove and its welded-in flat top cooking surface, a countertop for food prep and dishes, a table for eating, drinking coffee and shooting the breeze, and two corners – one with a bed and the other with a cot – for sleeping. Despite its small size, the cabin seems plenty spacious enough. Like newer homes, it hasn't had time to accumulate the inevitable clutter.

We head out for a quick ride behind the cabin to check a few traps and snares Jim has set nearby. Small winding trails connect a couple of tiny lakes. It's a neat little ride. Nothing's in the traps, and we return to the cabin to throw some more wood in the stove.

Having never built one of my own, I've always admired the craftsmanship that goes into log cabin making. Each log is fitted to its mate below and notched in the corners to help support the structure. The spaces between the logs are chinked with moss to keep the frigid air from entering. The roof is made live edge lumber slabs, probably from a chainsaw mill, covered in thick plastic and then a layer of dirt. A window by the dining table is covered with clear plastic – glass is likely to follow. It lets light in, at least when it's light out. The floor is covered in plywood – much nicer than the dirt floor trapping cabins often described in books. The door – or the opening, I should say – requires a step over a couple logs to get in. Jim knows from experience that these cabins tend to sink into the ground over time, so starting things out much higher is a way of compensating for that. The height of the cabin is impressive as well. Like me, Jim stands over six feet tall, and it's nice to have a cabin you can stand up in without having to worry about hitting your head.

The barrel stove is humping, and the heat pouring out of it is slowly soaking into the cold spruce logs and everything else inside the cabin. We go outside and begin unpacking the load in the fading light. Personal gear goes inside and to each of our respective corners, and food and trapping supplies to the other cabin. The other cabin, across the yard from the new one, serves as kind of a garage/utility shed/food storage area. It's considerably smaller, with a dirt floor and a short, sunken stature. I have to crouch down to get in and walk around. This cabin was originally built as a cache, and Jim and his brother Joe's main cabin was at the site which now sports the new one. When their main cabin burned many years ago they moved into this one and used it as their trapping cabin. It took a long time, but Jim finally rebuilt, and this little building is reverting to cache status. We unload the sleds as darkness sets in and return to the now warm cabin.

A bit of supper and a bit of skinning is on the evening's agenda. The two snared lynx we picked up on the trail are frozen solid. Their fur is so insulating that they'll be two days in the cabin before they're thawed enough to skin, I'm told. The lynx we caught alive in the trap is ready, though, and after dinner I observe in the lantern light while Jim skins, fleshes and stretches the pelt.

Story of a Trapline

We're up long before light. It'll be something to get used to for me. Seven seems like sleeping in, but when it doesn't get light until nine, and you're waiting for light to depart on the trap line, you have a couple of hours to kill. As we eat breakfast and drink cups and cups of instant coffee, I realize exactly how we're going to kill those hours, today and in the future. Jim has an incredible handle on the history of trappers and trap lines in this area, and I have an insatiable appetite for information like this. So we talk trapping.

Jim Firmin is from Alaska, but not the same Alaska we're in now. He grew up in Anchorage, where his parents ended up settling down after the military brought his father here from the Lower 48. Jim and his brothers spent a great deal of their childhood running around in the woods, hunting and exploring. When they were teenagers, a friend, Steve Zigman, suggested they try trapping. They tried it for a while, on the outskirts of Anchorage, but Jim was interested in something more.

At age sixteen or seventeen, Jim decided he wanted to get out of the big city and find somewhere to live in the woods. His older brother Joe knew someone in Fort Yukon, and in April of 1971 they visited the place and had a look around. By the end of summer, Jim and Joe had moved to Fort Yukon with dreams of establishing a trap line.

Joe befriended a native family, the Peters, who had a trap line up the Porcupine they weren't using, and the brothers were planning to spend the first winter out there, about forty miles from town. Folks in town were a little confused about these two boys from Anchorage, just out of high school, who were foregoing college or careers to go trapping.

Old man Philip Peter wasn't sure the boys were ready to go out that far from town, and the cost of a winter's outfit was a bit steep, so they ended up spending that first winter close to town. They rented a cabin in town for $15 a month and trapped out of Peter's cabin six miles from town. They passed the time cutting firewood to sell in town and trying to catch fur nearby. A fox and a lynx were all they had to show for those first couple of months, but the small catch didn't discourage them.

A couple of trips out to Jim Peter's trap line that winter, near the mouth of the Sheenjek, proved to be an eye opener. There was much more fur to catch once you got outside of that small, heavily trapped radius around town. Then, Jim spent a few months even farther out, at Shuman House, with Jimmy Ward from January to sometime in March that winter. Jimmy had taken over the trapline and cabin based at Shuman House from his father, legendary trapper Joe Ward, who immigrated from England in 1910 and spent his entire working life there as a professional trapper. Jimmy, in his late forties at the time, was one of the last in a long line of trappers who grew up in the bush and made their living out there harvesting fur.

"When I got to Fort Yukon," Jim would tell me "almost every adult male had spent time trapping." Today, he's one of the few left. As the price of fur got lower, it sped up the progression of families moving to town where there was a school, a hospital, and community. The men would still go out to the trap line, but would return to town more often, until eventually the idea of spending the entire winter out on the line was foreign to most. Everyone was coming in from the bush, and Jim and Joe were trying to get out there.

Jim putting in a trail snare

Jim and Joe ended up taking over the Peters' trap line on the Porcupine. They cut out old trails, built cabins, and harvested fur with the energy and enthusiasm of youth. Their first, and main cabin, was supposed to be built on the Peters' native allotment.

Native allotments, which still exist today, are parcels of land that Gwich'in natives were allowed to claim ownership of on Federal land they had historically used. The allotments were often claimed, but not surveyed, as was the case with this one. So they thought they were building on the allotment, in a nice stand of timber, but found out the allotment was a mile or so downriver from the new cabin. They got a permit for the cabin when the area became a National Wildlife Refuge, so all was good. They established a line up the lower part of the Sheenjek River, building a cabin there after carving out an agreed-upon boundary with Bill Russell, who trapped further upstream in some of Jimmy Carroll's old territory.

They started out trapping with dogs. The early 1970's were a time of change for transportation in the Alaska bush. Snowmobiles had just gone mainstream, and trappers were trading in their dog teams for machines. Just a few years before, when Richard K. Nelson did his work in Chalkyitsik, he noted that all trappers in the village had owned dogs in the past, but most were transitioning to snowmobiles, while often keeping their dogs for the first few years, 'just in case'. Young Jim and Joe Firmin saw all of the trappers transitioning to machines, but most complained and said they'd be going back to the dogs. "Heck," the young men figured, "dogs must be better." So they got dogs, and spaced line cabins at appropriate distances to accommodate the slower speed of dog travel. After one August where he cut summer work short to try and catch fish to feed his dogs for the winter, Jim realized it was time to switch to a snowmachine.

Joe married a native woman from Fort Yukon and began to settle down. He did some pipeline construction and worked odd jobs at first, and eventually became a pilot and established an air taxi business out of Fort Yukon. By then he said he wasn't going to trap anymore, but who can believe those words coming from a trapper? Jim was still single and ambitious. In addition to the line on the flats, he wanted to chase marten way up in the hills. He did a little background research, talking to some old timers with knowledge of the country, and was flown way up the Salmon Fork of the Black River, essentially the middle of nowhere, to a drainage that hadn't been trapped since the 1940's. He built a cabin and started trapping marten. It was incredible marten country, the stuff of dreams. One winter, when short of money and out of work, he caught over 100 marten in five weeks, running trap lines on foot.

Jim ended up marrying a member of the Peter family, Susan, who he remains with today. He'd spend summers working on a survey crew and other seasonal jobs and be flown out to the trap line in the fall, usually by his brother Joe. They continued to trap together on both lines. Jim's other brother Bill had an airplane too, and trapped the marten line with him as well, though he was a visitor, not a fixture in the area.

In 1992, Joe Firmin died in a plane crash while flying aerial surveys for Alaska Fish and Game. Not having a brother, I can only imagine how difficult it must have been to lose someone so close. Jim had begun to settle down by this time and was working more. Trying to maintain two trap lines was out of the question. He and Joe's widow turned the line up the Salmon Fork over to a trapper in Fairbanks, and Jim settled in to trapping the line on the Sheenjek and Porcupine, where we sit today.

Snake Trails

It's cloudy and mild, about zero degrees Fahrenheit. A light skiff of snow fell overnight, just enough to require a dusting off of the machines, toboggans and gear. We start up an old Tundra that Jim leaves in the cache. I'll be driving it today. It's the traditional 250 cc, single cylinder model, probably the most popular trapping machine in Alaska. The model is no longer made, having been replaced by the newer, and much bigger, 550 Tundra Jim drove here from town. Both have the advantage of being narrow, which is required for snaking through the tight trails through the bush that we'll be running now that we're off the river.

We get going, taking one of the winding trails through the woods, passing a trap here, a snare there. We break out onto a lake. It's long, narrow and winds back and forth in a gentle wave pattern. Like the others it has no name, but Jim calls it Snake Lake. Most traditional trap line trails in this country connect lake to lake, since travel across frozen lakes is far easier than winding through the woods, and reduces the miles of trail the trapper has to keep clear of freshly fallen trees each year. Lakes like this allow a trapper to cover a lot of ground in a short period of time. We stop at three or four places on the lake shore where Jim has set snares and traps for lynx or wolverine.

The little old Tundra isn't running quite right. Once it gets going it runs fine down the trail, but it won't idle, and threatens to die each time I let off the throttle a bit. When we stop, it takes a bunch of cranks on the pull cord to get it to start back up again. It's frustrating, but better than walking.

The old Tundra on a narrow trail

There's nothing in these traps, and we get to the end of the lake and climb the bank through the willows and onto another woods trail. We stop at each set location, clear snow from the traps, pack down fresh snow on snare trails, and adjust the height of snares where needed. Sometimes a trap's jaws are frozen to the ground.

We un-stick them from the ground and ensure they're ready to fire freely if a critter comes along.

Jim's foothold sets for lynx are about as simple as it gets. Seeing the first few took me by surprise, but now, as I help maintain the traps, I'm attracted by their simplicity and efficiency. Unlike coyotes, foxes or wolves, lynx are not trap shy. They don't seem to care about a bare metal trap sitting on top of the ground with no

Cleaning the snow from a cubby set

covering, and they'll step right on the pan without any hesitation. Wolverine seem to be the same way. These sets are simple. Lynx lure, usually a concoction made with a heavy dose of beaver castor, is smeared on the side of a tree. A foothold trap, usually a #3 or #4 coil or double long spring trap, is set on top of the ground (or packed-down snow) a few inches back from the tree. Several sticks are placed on each side of the trap to make a mini cubby, and a couple of guide sticks may be added to ensure the lynx steps in the right spot. As the lynx attempts to put its nose on the lure or rub its face against the tree, it steps on the trap and is caught. A long chain attached to the trap is secured by wrapping it around the tree and fastening it in place. A wolverine set is much the same as this, except that instead of lure, a piece of meat is wired to the tree for bait. The bait is attached firmly so that the wolverine has to work to try and pull the meat away, and has to keep planting its feet in the vicinity of the trap. At many wolverine sets, two traps are used. Though easy to catch, wolverine are difficult to keep caught. After being caught in the first trap, another paw in the second is added insurance.

We've reached the end of the line of traps Jim has set here, and now we're extending that line and making new sets. I'm mainly watching and learning. There isn't too much brush or downed trees in this trail. I believe Jim said he trapped here four years ago, so it's been kept up pretty well. There are traps hanging from trees at various locations throughout the line. These are places Jim has set traps and caught fur year after year. The bases of the trees are worn bare, and the small radii around them are clear of sticks, save for a few old ones used to construct cubbies. With such long and remote trap lines, I'd wondered how guys hauled so many traps around with them. We hadn't put many traps in the toboggans this morning, and now I know why.

In Maine, traps hung on trees out in the woods like this could meet a number of fates. The wet climate could rust them to an unusable state, a timber harvest operation could obliterate them, and a passing hunter or trapper could take them for his own. Those problems don't exist here in the Alaska bush. Unless a forest fire comes through, these traps could sit here for decades without being bothered. As an aside, I can't imagine many things more fascinating than finding traps hanging in trees from a trap line that was abandoned many years ago, its owner never to return. Jim has found them. Maybe someday I will as well.

This is fun stuff, cutting trail and making sets. I like working and I like progress. Before coming up here, I told Jim I wasn't worried about how much fur we caught. As long as I was doing something productive, whether that meant cutting firewood, clearing trails, making sets or collecting fur, I'd be happy. We break out of the forest and into a flat, brushy area. It's an old slough lake that's grown in with willows and is reverting to forest, becoming more difficult to keep a trail open in every year. The little tundra has died on me again. Jim is ahead of me and continues on as I repeatedly pull the starter cord. It's not the first time it's died, and it seems to start a little harder each time. This is getting more frustrating.

I pull a little harder. Too hard. It turns out you're not supposed to pull a starter rope all the way to its end. Guess I should have known that, but I've never had one break on me before. Until now. The handle and rope are in my hand and disconnected from the machine, and I'm in the middle of this meadow with Jim a couple hundred yards ahead of me on the trail. We still have a couple of hours of daylight left and I'm not going to sit here and wait for him to return. I put my backpack on and start walking down the trail. I figure I'll catch up and ride on his toboggan so we can keep extending the trail and setting traps. But before long I hear him coming back. It's decided we should get the old Tundra started and limp it back to the cabin. The trapping day is done. Bummer.

It takes twenty or thirty minutes to clutch start the machine and it runs all the way back. It'll get parked in the cache for future repairs and we'll have to use the big, wide Bearcat in its place. I feel bad. First full day on the line and I've ruined a sled. Quite a start. I help with some chores around the cabin, haul ice from the river, and cut and haul some firewood before dark.

Curtis Slough

We're up early, but as usual, daylight's late. There's a tiny skiff of snow on the ground and some flurries drifting about. Today we go up river. Even well after the sun should have risen, it's dark and gloomy on the Porcupine. We travel mostly along shore, traversing snow covered gravel bars on inside bends and out over the active river channel on slow stretches between riffles, where thick ice is more of a certainty. With quite a few miles and several large river bends behind us, we pull off the river on what looks like either a tributary, backwater or side channel.

It's called Curtis Slough, named after Waldo Curtis, a New Englander who came to the Fort Yukon area in 1897. Curtis was known as a good trapper who was smart with his money. He lived tough and didn't spend much. Some would joke that he just about lived off of muskrats and flour. When this area became crowded with trappers, Curtis moved further upriver to a place they call Howling Dog Canyon, where the Porcupine flows between steep rock walls. There are conflicting stories about how Howling Dog got its name. As one account goes, when trappers would boat upriver with their dogs following along shore, the tight canyon would force them to swim or climb the steep banks to continue upstream. Not wanting to do either, many a dog would stand there, howling as their owner moved farther and farther away. The simpler story? The wind blowing through the narrow canyon above Curtis' camp made a noise that sounded like a dog's howl.

We wind through the slough, stopping to check traps for lynx and wolverine. The banks are lined with willows and aspen, with spruces on the high banks. The willows seem to hold lots of hares, and their tracks cross the slough here and there. There are a couple of sets of lynx tracks too. Encouraging.

A pack of wolves had come through the last time Jim was up here, and it appears, based on large tracks covered with only the freshly fallen snow, that they've been back. He set four wolf snares off in a willow thicket, but no wolves have been near them. We round a bend and a small bull moose is out ahead of us, on a dead run for the trees. I feel a little bad for the moose, but mostly I'm amazed it's still alive with all of the wolf activity around. Whether it's hunters or four legged predators, moose seem to know they're a target in this country. I've yet to see one that isn't running away.

The next set, a foothold in a makeshift lynx cubby in the willows, provides excitement and letdown all at once. It's a mix of emotions we trappers are used to. A lynx has indeed visited this set, but so has the pack of wolves. All that's left is a furry foot in the trap, the remainder of the animal having been eaten or dragged off by members of the pack. We continue upstream, following the massive dog tracks as they crisscross from point to point to investigate different areas. Suddenly they all converge into one well-beaten path in the snow that leads up and over the stream bank to some sort of back channel. Hard packed trails wind through the trees along a hundred foot long stretch of willows. From the looks of it,

Jim figures there's a kill somewhere back there, probably a moose. It looks like my wolf trapping education is about to begin.

Wolves are the most difficult animal to trap. It's a statement I'm not too afraid to make boldly, as I don't think too many folks would argue it. You don't make it to the top of the food chain by being dumb, and wolves have an incredible ability to learn and sense danger. The gear used to catch and hold them is big, rugged and expensive. They cover large swaths of territory, and may or may not follow the same route when returning to an area. Anything that arouses suspicion has been known to throw an entire pack of wolves off to the side of a trail to avoid potential danger. They know enough to be dangerous while avoiding getting caught. Trappers seeking to catch wolves in any significant numbers must learn to match their wits.

Jim always keeps a few wolf snares on hand for situations like this, and we decide to set some. He gives me a brief bit of instruction and we each set two. They're massive wire loops suspended over the trail in places a wolf isn't likely to see them before walking through. It's almost surreal being able to make an attempt to catch a wolf, but I'm not too pumped about it. I know the odds are super low. I'll gladly settle for a few lynx, and perhaps a wolverine, but an opportunity like this can't be passed up, because you never know.

About a mile farther up the slough, I get the chance to set for wolverine. In a bench adjacent to the bank, an open area among the willows shows the tracks of multiple lynx and a wolverine. We employ a full on military strategy here, using all three of the tools we have in what looks to be a hot spot for furbearers. We make a cubby set baited with a lynx leg wired to a clump of large willows that serves as backing. We walk through small openings, making trails and setting snares. Finally, we pull a wooden box from one of the toboggans that we'd brought for this purpose. It's a makeshift wolverine cubby, in the shape of a square with an opening on the front and slots on the sides to hold the springs of a 330 bodygrip trap. I wire a lynx leg to the back of the box and set the big, deadly trap. I'm hopeful this will be the spot I catch my first wolverine.

330 set for wolverine

It's still overcast, but the snow has stopped falling and more of the afternoon light is reaching the slough. We check the last of Jim's sets and ride beyond them to look for sign. We pass two active beaver lodges. I can't help but think, for a brief moment, how I'd set these up. It quickly passes. Sure, it would be neat to catch Alaska beavers, but we've plenty of them in Maine. I focus ahead, looking for lynx tracks.

We've reached the end of the trail, so to speak. It's possible to go further, but there's a bit of ice that might be sketchy and we've probably covered enough ground anyway. We stop and discuss a plan of action. Jim suggests something I've been waiting for. We'll work our way back down the slough, setting traps on the sign we've seen, leap-frogging one another. Now that I've assisted for a couple of days, I'm thrilled about the prospect of setting traps on my own. And if that weren't enough to lift the mood, the sun peeks out of the clouds to shine bright on us for the first time since we left Fort Yukon.

Lynx tracks crossing the slough

I stop after just a short distance and analyze a lynx track that crossed the slough. It looks like it originated from way up the steep bank to my right. I grab the gear – a trap with chain, bait, lure, wire and some snares, and scramble up the steep bank through the soft snow. The bank flattens out to a bench about ten or fifteen feet wide, about twenty feet above the snowmachine and toboggan back on the ice. I walk a short ways to my left and come back, packing a trail where I'll set a lynx snare. Another one will hang in the trail shortly after the steep bank joins the flat bench. Now I go over to the right, looking for something distinct. There's a vertical bank a few feet high with a hollow area carved deep into it, under overhanging tree roots. It's almost like the entire bench I'm standing on became saturated with water and slumped off the hillside toward the slough, probably a long time ago judging by the size of the trees growing on it. I find it hard to imagine water could

The vertical bank set

get high enough to move a landform so massive, but I've learned that water has a way of surprising us at times. I have wolverine in mind, and for some reason I think this would be a neat place for one to be prowling around. I wire the bait – a lynx hindquarter – to one of the tree roots under the overhanging bank and set the trap under it and a short distance back. The trap is on bare dirt – a rarity in this land covered in snow. The area is just sheltered enough to keep the snow out but remains visible and accessible to animals. I place a few guide sticks and secure the trap to a nearby tree. I'm not sure if it'll catch anything, but it looks pretty awesome. I finish up the snares and slide down the steep bank.

I took way too long to make this set, so I'm looking to pick up the pace. I pass a spot Jim's already set, and pass his second stop just as he's arriving. Continuing around the bend, I find a low spot in the willows with lynx and rabbit sign around. I make a quick double snare trail set and move on. The next spot is another high bank, but not nearly as dramatic as the first. On a narrow bench I make kind of a walkthrough set beside the trail with a #3 coil spring trap and some lure rubbed against the tree. I set another trail snare and I'm gone. After a couple more locations, we've made it back to the end of Jim's previous line and it's time to call it a day.

We head down river, the sun low on the horizon, shining beautifully on the snow-covered channel and bringing me, for some reason, an incredible sense of joy. It hasn't been that long, but I do miss the sun when it's gone.

First Impressions

S itting down at the dinner table that night, we get a good chance to talk about my observations of the area and thoughts on the trip thus far. After spending a good part of my life thinking about being in a place like this, and most of the past year planning for this trip, I do have some thoughts after a couple of days.

First, the weather. It hasn't been super cold, but my initial nervousness about the weather and resultant detailed preparation has proven a success thus far. In fact, because it's been relatively mild, I've actually found myself a little overdressed at times. Some items have proven unnecessary, or more of a hindrance than help, like the ski goggles I brought, which constantly fogged and iced up on me. Other items, like the parka with fur ruff Jim lent me, have proven critical.

The snow machines themselves have been both a blessing and a curse. I've seen firsthand how important one is in getting around such a vast territory out here, but also how quickly the same machine that takes you to faraway places can just as easily leave you stranded in them.

I knew to expect the short days and long nights typical of winter above the Arctic Circle, but hadn't realized how much idle cabin time this would result in. There's more than ample time to complete the various tasks of cooking, cleaning and processing fur while it's dark. In fact, mornings and evenings are quite leisurely, sitting around drinking coffee or tea, listening to the radio, and talking trapping or area history. For the first couple of days I've reveled in this opportunity to relax. It's a big change of pace from my normal crazy-busy lifestyle back home. But I can clearly see how the slow pace could begin to drive me crazy over time. I like to be constantly moving, producing, progressing. I'm already trying to think of things I can do in the dead time, while also remembering the voice of my wife back home reminding me that this is a vacation, and it's okay – even necessary – to relax. Being a retiree, Jim has less trouble relaxing. He seems to have developed a balance of work and rest that suits him well out here.

Perhaps most notable of my observations is that of the land itself. The various pictures I'd seen in the preceding months apparently hadn't calibrated my sense of space that well. The Porcupine River, in person, is vastly larger and more expansive than I had imagined. Proportional to its great size, various features along the river are equally impressive. Many of the banks are twenty to thirty feet high and drop steeply to the water. Long, vast stretches of gravel bar are hidden under the blanket of snow, but reveal themselves almost eerily by the change in elevation and surreal feeling I get when the ground suddenly rises under me and the snowmachine and I are climbing in the middle of the river channel. Some of these bars are six to eight feet above the current water and ice level, while others are so close to the river's elevation that I don't even realize I'm traveling over land.

Crossing the Porcupine on snowmachine

The country surrounding the river, with its various lakes, sloughs and forest in all stages of succession, surprise me more than anything. This place is called the "Yukon Flats", an accurate depiction on a large scale, but on the ground level, it's anything but flat. Like the river, each lake, stream or slough is lined by banks – some steep, some gradual – and traveling the network of interconnected trails and lakes produces terrain as diverse as any other place, and perhaps more varying than most.

Even more impressive is the complexity of the wildlife habitat here. I pictured interior Alaska as a monoculture of stunted spruce and a simple, relatively barren forest floor. What I experience on the ground is the exact opposite. Each change in elevation, distance from the river, change in soil type, or boundary of historic flood or fire, is represented by a break in forest type. From willow covered benches and banks to aspen flats, to thick spruce regeneration, stunted spruce high ground and towering mature spruce lowlands, this place has it all. The accounts I've read about the productivity of this vast, historically rich fur producing area make perfect sense when seeing it on the ground. Each habitat type favors a certain species, and the edges – the transition areas between habitat types that are so common here – provide habitats that support different species in close proximity to each other, as well as additional species that thrive on the edges. It's a pretty neat place.

Young forest meets old

The Sheenjek

It's February 7, a Friday — not that the date matters much out here. It's mild for here today, a little below zero and cloudy with some sun. I've wanted to see the Sheenjek River since Jim first mentioned the line cabin he and Joe trapped from up there back in the 1980's. It's a pretty storied river as far as trappers go. James Carroll got his start there around the turn of the last century. In the 1920's, prospector turned trapper George Berglund and his family lived and trapped near the river's mouth. One of his daughters, Evelyn, wrote about her early childhood on the Sheenjek and other experiences in her book "Born on Snowshoes". Countless others have fished, hunted and trapped the river's corridor over the years. The old timers living at Shuman House on the Porcupine maintained a trail overland (about 15 miles as the crow flies) to the Sheenjek to fish for salmon. Their neighbor, Joe Ward, later used this trail as part of his trap line and built a cabin along it. Today, Tyler and Ashley Selden, made famous by the hit television show "The Last Alaskans," trap along the river's upper reaches.

Last night we had discussed options and attempted to make sort of a plan for where we'd spend the next day. When I heard the Sheenjek mentioned, I was all in. We're geared up and headed down the trail. The first couple of miles are pretty easy. Close to the cabin, these trails have been well maintained most every year. But there's a complication. After grounding the old Tundra, I'm now on the Bearcat, a larger and much wider machine. Its wide ski stance is designed for stability on open ground, and weaving along narrow trails in thick timber is not its strong point. Ahead on the newer Tundra, Jim has no trouble getting through, only occasionally stopping to cut a downed tree or move branches out of the trail. But with skis wider than the open space between many of the trees, I find myself stopped at many a spot Jim was able to cruise through. I hack away with the axe, clear a tree or two, and try to keep up.

We reach the end of a long, winding trail through pole sized spruces at the edge of a narrow lake. There's a fresh lynx track here and we stop to make a cubby set and place a couple of snares. We break onto the lake, zoom down it maybe a hundred yards, and climb the opposite bank into the opening created by another old trail. As the trail enters the tree canopy I see something peculiar hanging from a couple of spruce trees where Jim is stopped ahead of me. It's another stash of traps. I'd wondered again this morning how we'd be able to do much trapping with so little steel in our toboggans when we left. I'm a slow learner, but I'm catching on, as we pick out a few lynx traps and load them in. Here at the base of the tree where the traps hang, we make another lynx cubby, a few simple sticks on each side of the tree, a trap directly in front, and some cat lure rubbed on the tree trunk above the trap.

We continue along trails connecting lakes that wind through the spruce trees, stopping to make a cubby or snare set for lynx now and then. We even make a couple of snare sets on the main trail.

When given a choice, most critters will take the path of least resistance to get from point A to point B. Oftentimes that means lynx and other furbearers will follow the hard packed snowmachine trail for long distances before bailing off to hunt for rabbits in a particular thicket or patch of trees. Trappers take advantage of this tendency by setting snares right in the middle of the trail, using sticks or brush to direct the lynx to pass through a narrow opening in which the snare is hung. These trail snares are highly effective, but they're also a pain because they have to be taken down and reset each time you pass through on the trail. We'll be taking an alternate route back today, so we won't have to move these snares until the next check.

Trail snare for lynx

Many of the sets along these trails go in the same place year after year, as evidenced by the bare ground free of sticks and debris, and the rubbed-smooth surface of many of the trees, a clear indication that a lynx or wolverine was caught here in the not-too-distant past. Often there's even a trap hanging from the tree, ready to be put to work again when the time comes.

We break out onto another lake, a long one with a sharp bend on one end. On the other end we climb back into the woods, and the trail begins to look different. It seems to be fading. We go through a short stretch of large spruce trees and drop down a very steep bank onto a small channel that looks like a little stream or backwater slough. We plow through willows and alders and past a couple of abandoned beaver dams until the path ahead is too choked with brush to continue. We turn off the machines and start walking. I follow Jim up a high bank out of the brush and into a stand of spruce trees with a clean understory. He's looking for a trail. We walk a ways and he stops, pointing to a tree. There's a blaze on it, marked with an axe, put there by either him or his brother more than 30 years ago. He mentions running this trail with an old Skidoo Elan, the first machine they bought when giving up the dogs. We walk through the spruce flat for a ways, but the trail fades out. It's a futile exercise anyhow. The bank is too steep to climb with a machine in this spot. Sometime in the past three decades, high water and erosion must have carved away the old approach.

We return to the machines down in the slough and decide to scout a path ahead. The wall of brush is so thick that, combined with the deep soft snow that's settled into the slough under it, it's almost impenetrable. We slog through until the slough narrows down to a tight chute about twenty feet wide, with ten foot vertical cut banks on each side. Above the brush and the banks is a large area of open space. In that space, I'm told, is the Sheenjek River. I paw through brush and climb the left bank to a point of high ground to get a view. There it is. I'm pretty sure I'm only seeing part of the Sheenjek at this location. The map shows it splitting here, and the snow-covered channel I'm looking at is definitely too small to be the entire river. But it's still the Sheenjek.

Jim's upper cabin is on this river. It's probably ten miles away as the crow flies, maybe twenty by boat, but there's currently no way to reach it from here, and there hasn't been for many years. The Sheenjek had a different name in the old days – they called it the Salmon River. That's because the river supports robust runs of spawning salmon throughout much of its length. Part of the Sheenjek's appeal to salmon is its incredible abundance of groundwater seeping through the gravel, where salmon lay their eggs each year. The groundwater maintains a steady temperature – cool in summer, warm in winter – and keeps these spawning gravels from freezing solid throughout the brutally cold Arctic winters. Salmon eggs that hatch successfully complete a critical part of the life cycle that supports future generations and maintains a healthy population.

All this groundwater is problematic for travel though. Due to its groundwater influence, many parts of the Sheenjek don't freeze solid like most other rivers do, and the river can be a death trap for a trapper on snowmachine or dog team. So, long distance winter travel on the Sheenjek is out.

For some reason I can't get Jim's upper cabin, and the idea of visiting it, out of my head. Maybe it's the fact that it's so remote, or that it played such an important role in his early trap line, or just the idea that – as he told me earlier – there is no way we are going to be able to open up the old trail to get there during this trip. And in reality, that trail may never be opened again. It's a thought that gets to me, bothers me. I want to open the trail, see the cabin, and reestablish the old trap line loop between the two cabins. We stand there in the brilliant low sun for a few minutes before heading back to the machines. We've gone as far as we'll go in this direction.

With one last look up the Sheenjek, I think of our nearest neighbors upriver - way upriver - the Seldens. Tyler Selden was born and raised in farm country, Nebraska. He and his brother spent their childhood outdoors, hunting, fishing, trapping and roaming the fields. But from a young age Tyler dreamed of wilderness. He went to college in northern Minnesota, close to the northern forests that stretch into Canada, trying to feed that dream. But it wasn't enough. Tyler met Ashley in school. His dream of living in the wilderness was contagious, and she was on board. Shortly after they married, the couple departed for Alaska with a dream, but not much else. First landing in Anchorage, they moved wherever work could be found, from tourist trap coastal towns to a truck stop on the northern haul road. Despite moving a couple thousand miles, the Seldens realized they weren't any closer to the wilderness lifestyle they'd envisioned when reading about folks like Heimo Korth, who spent most of their life in the remote Alaskan bush.

In a stroke of luck, Tyler found a job in Fairbanks with expert log home builder and trapper, Bill Kisken. It was an important first step into a network of people in the Fairbanks area whose lives revolved around remote trap lines. They began asking around. One person knew another, who knew another, who may have a trap line for sale.

Unlike in Canada, there are no registered trap lines in Alaska. Most land in the state is publicly owned, and anyone who purchases an Alaska trapping license and abides by the proper regulations has equal right to trap it, technically. But there's an unwritten rule, a code, that almost all Alaskan trappers respect and live by. If someone goes through the effort of finding an area that isn't claimed by someone else, builds a cabin, cuts trails, and establishes a trap line, that line is respected by others as though it were private property. Others may hunt, fish or recreate there, but they will not trap it.

This unwritten code allows folks to 'own' their own trap line, a concept that's allowed countless young men and women the opportunity to fulfill dreams of starting from nothing and developing an honest living harvesting fur and carrying on a way of life that most Americans have no interest in, but a select few can't imagine going without. So, many people 'own' trap lines in Alaska, and occasionally an owner, usually due to old age, will decide to sell. By selling a trap line, the owner isn't conveying title to land, or even legal right to use the land. They are selling the cabins, equipment on site (which usually includes a pile of traps and an old snowmachine or two) and their promise to trap that area no more. Trap lines are bought and sold regularly in Alaska. For a young trapper looking to get started, buying a trap line is often their best bet.

Jim had heard Tyler was asking around about trap lines for sale, and figured his friend Ron Bennett might be interested in selling his line up the Sheenjek. It included a couple of old cabins, a Skidoo Elan and a bunch of traps stashed up in the hills somewhere. Ron had trapped there for several years, but when fur prices dropped he moved on to other business ventures, including guided viewing trips for tourists seeking the aurora borealis (the northern lights) in winter time. From the stories I've heard, a book could probably be written on Bennett alone. Most people didn't think he would sell, but he did.

Tyler and Ashley scraped together every last penny they had and purchased the Sheenjek trap line. Since then, they've spent most every winter up there, flying or boating up in the fall and returning to town by late winter or early spring. In keeping with tradition, they run their trap lines with a dog team, which they feed primarily with salmon they net from the river. They spend summers working and gardening out of a small cabin on the outskirts of Fairbanks, all in an effort to ensure they have the resources to return to their life in the bush each fall.

Running a trap line the way the Seldens do is an incredible sacrifice – both financially and emotionally – that most aren't willing to undertake these days. The isolation from society – no internet, no phones, no visitors – and the financial challenges brought on by today's dismal market value for wild fur compounds the challenges. Just chartering a plane from Fairbanks to a bush cabin can cost in excess of $1500. It can take many weeks to catch enough fur just to pay the cost of getting there. And there's no retirement plan in the trapping industry. It takes a special person to live such a lifestyle. The sacrifices can be brutal, but the rewards are priceless.

We leave the Sheenjek and backtrack to the lake that serves as a hub for trails going in several directions. We return to the trail we'd abandoned two days earlier, when I'd broken the old Tundra. The old trail is in decent enough shape to be cut out, Jim says, and there's plenty of daylight remaining. We reach the end of our old tracks quickly – it's a short distance, and all the traps we'd set are empty – and continue cutting trail and setting traps. We're working through high ground that supports a stand of large spruce trees, interspersed with smaller, pole sized trees. There are a few sloughs or lakes here and there, but they're noticeably older, holding little water and now choked with brush and the beginnings of a new forest. To me, the area looks more like classic Alaska marten habitat than anything I've seen yet. We'd actually seen a marten track when on this trail two days ago and Jim had made a leaning pole set for it. I mention to Jim that it looks like marten country here.

"Back in the '80's when there were marten in the Flats, this is one of the places we'd catch them" he says. He's told me of one year he and Joe caught about 80 marten on this line. Today, one set of tracks is about as close as you can get to catching a marten here. So what happened? It's hard to say. Lynx and marten don't mix, and the Flats have traditionally been dominated by lynx. Lynx populations fluctuate wildly throughout the species' range on a fairly predictable ten year cycle, coincident with snowshoe hare populations, and you might expect that marten would move into the flats during each low in the lynx cycle, but based on local trapper observations over the years, that hasn't proven out. Marten seem to move here in very infrequent waves separated by what might be decades. Philip Peter, who trapped this line in and around the 1940's, spoke of catching marten here. The Firmins experienced the marten wave of the '80's. But since then, the marten haven't been back here in any meaningful numbers. They remain in the high hills, far off in the distance.

The creek has a name, but I won't mention it

We move through the spruce-covered high ground, cutting trail and setting traps, and begin a long, gradual descent to a creek. We drop down a bank to the snow-covered ice, which is flat at creek level, but exists in broken, almost vertical sheets along the bank. The water level in this creek was apparently several feet higher when it first froze. Most of the ice has since sunk with the falling water, but the sheets that cling to the bank remain as evidence of its former state. We zip downstream for a ways as I admire the mature spruce-lined banks. To me the place looks a lot like home in northern Maine, with one striking exception. A hundred years ago, this place looked exactly as it does today, and a hundred years from now, it will remain so. There are no people, no towns, no machines building roads and cutting trees, no mills to turn them into lumber and paper. This place is still wild.

The creek has a name, but I won't mention it. It appears to have been named after a person, but despite all my searching, I can't find any documentation of the source. Probably some trapper, a long time ago, had a cabin along here somewhere. He probably kept no diary, wrote no book. If he did, it hasn't survived.

Above the almost vertical ice sheets on the right bank is an abandoned beaver lodge, with the old den entrance now a hole on the side of the bank. Jim suggests I toss some bait in the hole and set a 330 bodygrip trap in front of it for wolverine. I'm thrilled to do so. Finished up, as I stand atop the high bank, enjoying the beauty in what's probably the most remote place I've been to thus far, I pose a question to Jim that's been rattling around in my brain in some form or another all day.

"In the past twenty years, how many people would you say have been to this spot?"

There's no immediate answer. He has to think about it for a bit. Twenty years is a long time.

"About four or five" he says.

We're at the end of the current line. The long trail north of here, part of the old line, has likely not seen a soul in the past twenty years. Or even thirty. Imagine that. The beauty of this place is that it's so vast and so untraveled that just being here I feel a strange sense of ownership – on a trap line where I'm just a guest for a couple of weeks.

"In the past twenty years, how many people have been to this spot?"

It's getting late and we get started again, backtracking our way on the miles of winding trail and narrow lakes, back to the cabin.

The moon is out this evening, big, bright and beautiful. Back in the cabin, it's time to process some fur. After hanging in the warm cabin for a couple of days, the two lynx we caught in snares on the way in finally look thawed enough to skin. By lantern light, I watch while Jim pelts the first one. It's a unique process done with a unique tool. If I were home, I'd rough skin the critter, peeling the pelt off quickly, fat and all, and put it on a fleshing beam to scrape the fat off before drying. This method is different. Using just a knife and a fleshing tool, Jim can accomplish the same outcome in a single step. He makes his opening cuts with the knife, and instead of peeling the skin off the conventional way, he uses his fleshing tool – a unique scraper that his brother carved from the leg bone of a cow moose decades ago – to separate fat from skin as he peels the pelt down. When done, he's left with a clean lynx skin that needs almost no fleshing. It's ready to be put on the stretching board to dry.

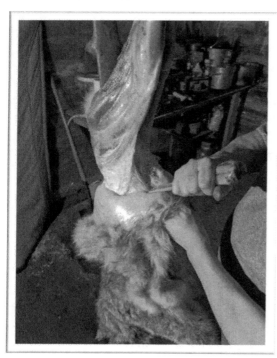

Skinning lynx with a moose bone

I'm supposed to do the next lynx, but it's not quite as thawed out as we thought, and I'm feeling pretty played out, so we leave it for tomorrow. I'm coming down with a cold. It's been a few days, about the proper incubation period, since I was on the flight to Seattle crammed up against that woman with the cold. Though I'd hoped otherwise, there really was no way of avoiding catching that one. I take some pills and head to bed.

Cutting Trail

I t's another calm morning around 5 below zero with mostly
clear skies. The cold I started feeling last night is full blown
now – sore throat, stuffy nose, and a real lack of energy. Today
we're going in a different direction. Each day we discuss our options
and make plans. Like I tell Jim, I only have one real motivator in
determining what we do. As long as we are making progress on
something, I'm happy. That may mean cutting trail, it may mean
setting traps, or even cutting firewood. The only thing I don't want
to do is sit around and do nothing.

We cross the Porcupine and climb the twenty foot tall bank to
an aspen flat. Today we'll open up another old trail. This one is
short, but important. It's one of the many overland trails that cut
off bends in the river, which snakes back and forth so wildly it can
flow for long stretches without making much forward progress
toward its destination. By opening the trail, we'll shave a couple
miles off our next trip upriver and have another area to set and
check traps on the way through.

This trail is loaded with downed trees, and the chainsaw we
brought along gets more work than the rest of the tools. Low on

energy from my cold, I wonder if it's really worth the effort to make the shortcut, and start to understand how easy it is to let the wilderness reclaim these old trails after a couple of years without maintenance. Like Jim has told me more than once, it's easy to cut trails from the kitchen table, looking at the map. But this? This is work.

Opening up an old trail

"Long trap lines aren't found or discovered, they're built." Legendary interior Alaska fur buyer and trapper Dean Wilson made that statement years ago, and it still rings true today. An Alaska trapline, for the most part, is a base cabin and a series of line cabins connected by a large network of trails. Cutting and maintaining trails is one of the most crucial and labor intensive jobs on the trap line.

Making a trail from scratch requires planning, navigation and quite a bit of grunt work. The first step in the process is deciding where on earth you want it to go. A trapper might select a general location based on terrain, land and water features, known abundance of furbearers, adjacent trap lines, or a number of other factors. Once the general location is decided upon, it's then a matter of finding the best route to, and through, the country. Best doesn't always mean most direct. Often the best route involves a winding, zig-zaggy trail that follows the path of least resistance and requires less cutting to open and maintain.

Watercourses are often the easiest routes of travel, but they do present their own issues. Backwater lakes and sloughs, which are often parts of ancient river channels, as well as active rivers and creeks, can make for easy travel but can also be a nightmare if thin ice and heavy snow result in overflow. Overflow – or more simply, water on top of the ice – can be the traveler's worst nightmare, resulting in stuck machines and wet, frozen feet. No fun. But when ice conditions are good, these travel routes are clear of obstructions and, mercifully, require no maintenance.

A trapper often ties watercourses together by cutting connecting trails between lakes, usually in places where they come closest together. When traveling by river, trails often cut off long river bends to save time and fuel. These overland trails can have the added benefit of being great places to set traps, as they get off the river a ways and into more forested habitat, and a lot of animals traveling the river may use them for the same purpose as the trapper who cut them out. In some places river ice just isn't safe enough for consistent travel, and trails may avoid travel over the ice and stick to the forest. Getting on and off portage trails can be tricky, since the shortest distance between two river bends usually occurs on cut banks where water actively erodes the soil, making what are usually pretty steep grades to climb and descend. Often trappers will check these places out in the summer or fall when their tops can be dug down with a shovel and be made passable with a

On the trail

snowmachine. Then, with a little speed and courage one can navigate the steep banks until a trail of hard packed snow makes it a breeze.

There's no getting around it, cutting trails through the woods is just plain work. Forest types vary in the arctic, ranging from young, brushy riparian willow, cottonwood and alder growth, to all stages of spruce, small and stunted to large and towering. The brushy areas are pure monotony, hacking away at the seemingly countless small stems with axe, machete or brush saw, and every year or two these small branches continue to crowd the trail and need to be brushed back again. In larger, older growth you can often wind through the big trees in the open understory, but when one of those big spruces comes down, chainsaw work is the only quick way to get through.

Once a trail is cut, maintaining it is a lifelong task – at least for the life of the line. Some years it's easy. The occasional tree falls across the trail and the slow encroachment of brush can be taken care of routinely. Other years, heavy snowfall and/or wind can bring what seems like the whole forest down on a trapper's trails. That's when keeping the trap line open gets to be a pretty depressing task.

Some years fire burns through a trap line and changes the forest completely. Cutting trails can be futile in such places. The standing dead burned trees can fall on trails faster than they can be cleaned up. Plus, a burn can result in the virtual disappearance of furbearers for years. Many trappers give up on a trail, or an entire trap line after a burn.

Other times, trails seem to be almost maintenance free for years, even decades. If a trail is followed by moose and other game it often stays relatively open with little work. Stands with healthy trees, well drained soils and sheltered conditions may experience few blowdowns. Some trails, or at least large portions of them, can be followed decades after trappers abandon them.

What's the best time to cut trap line trails? Some might say "whenever you can get around to it," but most trappers agree that late winter during a year of high snowfall is one of the worst times to cut line trails. Not only is wading through the snow tough work, many of the obstacles buried in the deep snow may be missed, and prove a hindrance in future periods of low snow. Then again, if you're done trapping for the season, the long, warming days of March and April can make for good, productive trap line cutting conditions.

Old Joe Ward, who ran long lines in the Yukon Flats for decades, used to walk all of his trails in the summer to maintain them and ensure they were ready for the next season. Joe was all business, and when trapping season came, he intended to spend his time setting and checking traps, not cutting trail. It must have been serious work walking around all of the lakes and streams, and clearing trails with axe and hand saw, but trapping was a profession back then, and a full time job for most of the old timers.

That leads to the most important part of cutting trails – you can set traps! In the act of cutting trail, you're carving your very own trap line out of the wilderness. Like the old timers told Jim back in the day, "You cut a trail, and it's yours." As common courtesy and a standard of practice, trappers almost never used others' line trails to travel, and never trapped on them. So, short of having title to the land, cutting a trail is the trapper's route to a trap line in bush Alaska. Freedom and ownership takes work, but if you want it bad enough, such a line can still be had today.

A Lynx

Battle worn, we finally break back out to the river. In the couple of miles of trail, we've seen hardly a lynx track, and only set traps in a couple of spots. We continue upriver to check our traps at Curtis Slough. We part ways shortly after entering the slough. Jim is headed to check and maintain wolf snares, and I'm looking over the traps we set for lynx the other day. I'm somewhere between the wolf snares and the end of our line, in a place on the right bank where we'd seen a lot of sign earlier. I approach the set and see movement. A lynx!

There it is, caught by the front foot in a #4 double long spring trap, looking at me. It's my first lynx. I'd set the trap, I'd checked the trap, and now I'm going to dispatch the animal. I find a pole and attach a snare from the snowmachine box to the end of it. I'm so nervous I don't stop for close-up pictures. I try to remember how Jim did this the other day. Quick, efficient, humane. Get it done and then I'll think about pictures. I slip the snare over its neck and pull it tight, then lift the cat into the air. After a brief struggle it's dead, and I move in close to take pictures and admire the animal.

My heart is racing. The feeling of regret in making the kill, the pride of accomplishment, and the rush of excitement from the entire process culminate into what feels like some elevated understanding of what I'm doing and why I'm out here. I think this is what ethicist and Cornell professor James Tantillo calls 'tragic wisdom'. I've experienced it before, and will likely do so until the day I die. It's an important part of life.

Low light on the Porcupine

I head back downriver, the brilliant sun shining on my face. I'm anxious to show my catch to Jim, but we've agreed to meet back at the cabin, so it'll be a while yet. I take my time. At the mouth of the slough there's a cabin perched atop a high, windswept bank overlooking the vast Porcupine. I park the machine and scramble up the twenty or thirty feet to check it out. The view here is incredible. The cabin is unlocked. It's a simple structure, maybe 10'x10' or 12'x12', with two beds, a small barrel stove, a table, a propane cook stove and a pair of bunny boots. While it isn't much, and cold air pours through the cracks between the logs, a structure like this could save your life if you broke down or fell through the ice nearby. Later Jim tells me the cabin belongs to Dickie Strum. The name sounds familiar. In his collection of stories about life on the Porcupine River, "Kaiiroondak: Behind the Willows" Richard Martin tells of a Charlie Strum, his brother in law and short time trapping partner, who also had a trading post upriver.

I'm back around dusk, and there's a beautiful, super bright full moon rising. It's hard to capture with pictures, but I try.

Gy-Roo

A nother day dawns with the temperature hovering around zero degrees. This time it's overcast with light snow falling. The area seems to get a lot of these light snowfalls. They often deposit only a quarter to a half an inch of snow – just a dusting. It's enough snow to make a mess on every surface, but not enough to warrant a full scale snow removal effort. We cover the machines with pieces of light canvas and cover or tip the toboggans over each night, which helps. The dustings cover branches on the travelways, ensuring snow falls down your neck when clearing trail or passing through tight spots. But the light dustings of snow can be good for the trapper too. They help you pinpoint fresh animal tracks and determine the age of older ones.

Despite the diverse habitat, this is interior Alaska, essentially an arctic desert, and it's hungry country. Animals can be few and far between, and are often absent from large areas for long periods of time. With no big snowfalls to obliterate tracks, sometimes you can be driving down a slough and see a dozen sets of lynx tracks that were all made two or three weeks before. You set traps, thinking the lynx are there, but they're gone. The snow dustings help with this. No fresh tracks a few days after a dusting is a sure indication that you're in a ghost town, at least for the time being.

We leave the cabin and turn off the trail a short ways in, onto yet another old trail I wasn't aware of. We skirt a small lake, cutting brush and setting a few traps along the high bank that parallels it. The trail breaks out onto a high bank overlooking the Porcupine. It's another beautiful spot. I notice a "Private Property" sign facing the river. It seems so incredibly out of place here, outside of the fringes of civilization. We're at a place called 'Ty-Roo-A' in Gwich'in. Jim's not sure what it means in English. It's the site of his wife's family's native allotment, claimed during the 1970's era Federal Government program that allowed natives to claim up to 160 acres of land where they could demonstrate a history of use. Susan's grandmother claimed this spot. It was part of the family trap line, and they would camp here when hunting and trapping muskrats on the surrounding lakes each spring. It's also the plot of land a young Jim and Joe thought they were building their trapping cabin on all those decades ago, before it was staked and surveyed.

We descend the long steep bank and cross the Porcupine, headed downstream. We're going to a place called 'Gy-Roo' in Gwich'in. Not sure what that one means either. It's a slough lake that runs parallel to the river for a long ways in a direction we haven't yet been on this trip. The climb from the river to the upper bench and the old trail to 'Gy-Roo' is a tricky one. There's a little climb to a floodplain bench, and a short approach to a seemingly vertical ascent to the flat high ground above the river. There's a sharp turn in there too. In all, it's probably only a thirty foot vertical climb over a couple hundred foot stretch, but getting through is like trying to negotiate an obstacle course.

We walk through the low bench and use axes to clear out sticks and logs deposited by the river during flood stage. We pack down a path and get the machines. It takes a little doing, but Jim clears the high bank with the Tundra. I'm not so lucky with the Bearcat. The last sharp turn in the trail doesn't allow me the speed and momentum I need to get up the hill. Halfway up I'm stuck. I unhook the toboggan, back down, turn around and make another run. And another. And another. Finally I make it through. I walk

Jim on his wife's family Native Allotment

back and get the toboggan, dragging it up the slope. By the time I get to the top I'm just about spent, and we've hardly even gotten started!

This high ground aspen and willow flat starts out pretty open, but as we leave the river the trees are thicker and the bushes grow closer together. Jim snakes through these with the Tundra quite easily. With the wide ski stance on my machine I often skirt a bush on one side while clipping one with the ski on the other. I mow them over and they spring back up behind me.

Now we're into an old overgrown trail and we're cutting more than riding. This one hasn't been used for a very long time. To get through with my machine I often have to stop at a spot Jim whizzed by and clear an extra tree or two to get the wide skis through. That puts him quite a ways ahead of me and I work to keep up. In places we lose the trail completely and wade back and forth through the soft deep snow looking for an opening or an old blaze on a tree. We find it again, and Jim uses his axe to make additional blazes to help mark the way for future travel.

Struggling across this flat, I'm beginning to realize that the image of cutting trail I had in my head was nowhere near what it's turned out to be in reality. One of the goals I had when coming out here was that I wanted to help Jim clean trail. I'd thought it was a shame that all these old trails were growing in and would soon become unusable like the many other trails abandoned by trappers long ago. The trouble is, I have no idea where the trails go, or how to find and follow them. That puts Jim in the lead, keeping on the trail and doing about 90% of the work. When he stops to clean a downed tree, I have just enough time to catch up, get off the machine, and walk up to where he's finishing up and he's ready to go again. I'm offering little to no help, but my enthusiasm and desire to see new ground is pushing him to work at clearing more trails. I'm working the old guy pretty hard, and I'm starting to feel kind of bad about it.

After a long battle with the brush-tangled flat, the ground drops away below us and suddenly we're in 'Gy-Roo'. It's an old slough, shallow and brushy, and very narrow. We travel its navigable length, which amounts to a couple of miles or so before the brush gets too thick, and scout for places to set traps and snares. Judging from the tracks, there appears to be quite a few lynx and rabbits here. We make some snare sets and some baited cubbies with footholds. After going such a long distance it would be nice to loop back to the river. It's not far from us at all, but there's no trail, and we aren't going to open one up today. We backtrack yet again.

Back on the Porcupine the day isn't over yet, so we zip over to a slough where we'd seen some lynx and wolverine tracks earlier. In the woods a ways, Jim sets a couple of trail snares for lynx and I make a baited cubby set with a 330 bodygrip trap for wolverine. It's a nice way to end the day. My cold has caught up with me, and I'm feeling pretty worn out for a young guy. I'm guessing Jim's feeling as bad or worse, so I try not to complain.

Near the mouth of the Sheenjek

Our recent trail cutting reminds me of Joe Ward, who ran long trap lines and maintained more than 300 miles of trail north of here. Ward was an Englishman, born in Blackburn, Lancashire, England. He worked as a gardener until immigrating to the United States with a friend around 1910. Ward spent some time working in the lumber camps of California. He wanted to head north, and found himself first working in a greenhouse in Whitehorse, and later floating down the Yukon to Dawson and sinking shafts in area creeks with three other gold prospectors. The four made their way down the Yukon into the United States, past Fort Yukon and up the Porcupine, destined for the hills on a prospecting mission. They made it to Shuman House and visited with the Herberts, the family who lived there, who said they'd be froze in soon. Sure enough, the river froze up the next day, putting an end to their upstream progress. The men went a couple of miles above Shuman House and built a cabin to spend the winter. One by one the other men left, but Joe Ward stayed right there, at that same cabin site, for most of the rest of his life.

Ward attributed the kindness of his accidental neighbors, the Herberts, for a great deal of his success. Joe Herbert taught Ward how to trap, shared his knowledge of the area, hunted with him, and offered him trapping ground. They became good friends, and Ward later referred to the family as "the finest people in the world." In Fort Yukon in those early days, Joe was approached by a friend, Dickie (Richard) Martin, who told him that Ellen, a native woman living in the village, wanted to marry him. Joe thought that would be fine, so they were quickly married and headed upriver on a honeymoon – trapping on the Porcupine. They would remain married for more than 50 years.

Joe Ward was a regimented man and a hard worker. Over time he single-handedly developed what was probably the most extensive trap line in the entire area. He built lines in circuits to avoid back tracking and put together a series of eleven line cabins for overnight stays. He'd travel about twenty-five miles a day with his dog team.

When trapping season started, Joe was ready to go. He walked his trails in the summer to clear out brush and deadfalls. He cut firewood and had enough split and dried wood at each cabin for the season's use well in advance. His hard work, preparation and discipline were a big part of his success. He'd leave at a certain time, stop to eat at a certain time or place, and so on. Everything was planned. When he got done at the end of the day, Joe would have a 'gear cabin' to pull his sled into, making it easier to organize gear and keep the sled clean of snow. You might think of it as a wilderness trapper's garage.

Joe trapped primarily for mink, fox, marten and lynx, and put up big numbers. One year, during a peak in the lynx population cycle, Ward caught 275 lynx, more than anyone else in the Fort Yukon area. During the spring he'd trap and shoot muskrats in the various lakes that dotted his trapline country. One spring he harvested 3,000 'rats. Catches like this allowed Joe Ward to make a full time living trapping for half a century, a feat that very few trappers throughout history could ever lay claim to.

The Wards would make the long journey down the Porcupine to Fort Yukon once in the winter, for Christmas and New Year's, and once in the summer, where they'd stay for about a month, visiting friends and resupplying, before returning home to their cabin near Shuman House.

Joe was well respected among the Fort Yukon trapping community, and made a great many friends during his decades there. He and Ellen couldn't have children, but they adopted Jimmy, one of James and Fannie Carroll's children, and raised him out in the bush. Jimmy took over his father's trap lines as Joe got older, slowed down, and eventually moved to Fort Yukon to spend his final years. Jimmy was still trapping at Shuman House when a young Jim Firmin came into the area and stayed with him in the 1970's. He was one of the last of the old timers, those who'd grown up spending their lives on the land, to whom town was just a place to visit, and the bush was their home. Joe Ward's trap line is empty today. The trails are grown in, the cabins rotted to the ground or burned in forest fires. The old home cabin site on the Porcupine is a clearing with some remnants of past occupation. Most wouldn't know there was ever anything there.

Alone

It's the tenth of February. Jim has been talking about a trip to town for the past couple of days, and today he plans to make the run. We're a little low on injection oil for the snowmachines, and it's a chance to bring up more fuel, food and other minor supplies. With colder weather in the forecast, he figures he can get to town, gather things, spend the night and make it back tomorrow afternoon before the cold spell hits. I'll stay here and run the traps.

Jim is loaded up and ready to go. We start both sleds and I accompany him downriver for the first couple of miles. We have a set in a clearing a little ways back from the river. A wolverine visited it the other day, stole the bait and wasn't caught. I bring a box and a 330 to set beside the existing foothold cubby set. We wave goodbye as Jim heads toward town and I turn in to the trail that leads to the wolverine set. I put the box in place, bait it and set the 330 in the entrance. It looks good. I make some improvements to the foothold set as well, and head back upriver.

I'm at the cabin, machine off, and all is dead silent. This is it. In a few hours I'll be the only human being within about 40 miles of here. I'm strangely excited by this revelation. As much as I've enjoyed trapping with Jim this past week, there's part of me that has always dreamed of running a remote wilderness trapline on my own, and today I'll be as close as I've ever gotten to experiencing it. Despite being a pretty social person, I've forever joked with my wife and others that I could easily spend a month or two alone in the bush. I'm not sure if I'll ever get the opportunity to find out if it's true. For now, a day or two will have to do.

Already geared up for the day, I start the machine back up and pull onto one of the spoke trails radiating out from the cabin yard. I'm running a couple of small lines we set up two days ago, and some of Jim's existing sets we checked on at the same time. Two days isn't a long time for fur to find its way into traps in country like this, but I'm excited nonetheless. Just the idea that I might catch something has me pumped up. I wind through the pole spruces, checking a few traps along the trail, drop onto a long narrow lake, and look for the trail on the opposite bank. I'm headed for the spot where we had a lynx set on the bank above the lake, in the clump of large spruces where a stash of traps had been hanging. I leave the lake, climb the bank and barely reach the top when I see it. I shut the machine off before getting too close. In the willows just ahead is a lynx in our trap, looking at me. It had been caught in the pen set made at the base of a tree a few feet away, and dragged the toggle stick we'd wired the trap to into the willows until it was hung up. The cat is fairly well blended into its surroundings as it looks at me with seemingly little fear. I can hardly believe it. Only a few traps in and I've got a lynx! From the toboggan I pull out the pole and snare setup that I used to dispatch my first lynx the other day. I take a quick picture at a safe distance, and move in and do the deed. I admire the fur. It's another beautiful animal, one that I feel privileged to harvest. I put the cat in the toboggan, wrapped in a section of light canvas to protect the fur from damage while it rides along. I remake the set and get going, wondering what the rest of the line will bring. I have a lot of traps yet to check!

Lynx cubby near a stash of traps – connected!

I move through the mostly wooded section of trail, checking sets here and there and moving a couple of trail snares out of the way as I pass through, resetting them behind me. I leave the woods and emerge onto Snake Lake. We have several places along the lake's shoreline where Jim has had sets out for quite a while this season. Many of the area lynx have probably been harvested here, so I'm not super hopeful that I'll find a catch in these, but it's still exciting to check them. There's a bit of snow to be packed down on our foot trails, traps that need to be cleaned of snow to ensure their proper functioning, and snare heights to be adjusted.

In one small cove I pack the fresh, fluffy snow down on the hard base of the trail, step over a snare and check a pen set made for wolverine. There's nothing here. I pull the trap up out of the ground. After a time, many of these traps start to freeze down, so picking them up and re-positioning them can help keep them free and ready to fire if stepped on. I can't remember if Jim had another set in this spot. I look to my left down a well worn trail and something looks out of place. I walk closer. It's a lynx! Caught in a snare, the cat wrapped itself around a log, expired quickly, and is elevated off the ground, frozen solid and covered in the skiff of fresh, powdery snow. Number two!

The snare is bent out of shape and frozen onto the lynx carcass, so I'll have to get another one from the machine. I detach the cable and haul the lynx back to the lake and deposit it beside the other in the toboggan. I'm beyond excited. This is amazing. I remake the snare set, get back on the machine and continue down the lake.

The next and final leg of today's trap check journey is the long trail through the woods that terminates at the creek. I start down it, winding my way through, stopping to maintain sets here and there. I see a couple of fresh lynx tracks, the second and third set I've seen for the day. It's encouraging to see sign on our lines, but animals that pass through don't always get caught. Sometimes a track will appear on the trail, follow it for a while, and leave into a thicket of trees, never to appear again. They come and go, reminding me that our trap sets aren't the center of the cats' universe. Snowshoe hares are.

I check the pole set that Jim made for the one marten whose tracks we'd seen days ago. It hasn't been touched. But a short ways beyond the set, not far from where I'd broken down with the old

Tundra, is a fresh set of marten tracks. It crosses back and forth on the trail several times, hunting in the old slough that's grown into a brushy meadow. I stop at a clump of willows the marten had passed within a few feet of, and decide to make a set for it. Since the marten didn't climb the pole set, I figure, maybe it'll have some interest in food on the ground. I break off sticks from the willow clump and make a small pen that terminates at the base of the clump. I chain a #1.5 long spring trap, just the right size for a marten and riding along in the toboggan for just this purpose, to one of the willow trunks and set it at the entrance of the pen. I wire some meat to the back of the cubby, several inches off the ground, add a little lure, and the set is done.

I move along through the meadow, stopping once to make a wolverine set at the base of another willow clump. Jim has caught wolverines in this area before, and we don't have many sets for one here. Plus, I have a couple of extra traps and a chunk of bait with me, so I might as well use it. The trail leaves the meadow and ascends into the older growth spruce country that struck me as classic marten habitat when we'd set it up. I dip into a small, ancient slough, climb back out into the spruces up a small hill, and come face to face with lynx number three.

It's a surreal scene, one that I'll think back on for a long time. A clean forest floor, two large spruce trees and a wildcat standing between them, looking, it seems, directly into my soul. I take a little extra time for pictures. I don't want to forget this one. I dispatch the lynx, put him in the sled and move on. At the end of the trail is the creek. I drop onto the ice and buzz over to check the wolverine cubby set in the abandoned beaver house. It's untouched. I'm not sure what time it is, but I'm sure I have plenty of daylight, so I decide to venture up the creek a ways further than where Jim and I turned around. I go around a bend and motor through soft, powdery snow that hasn't been traveled on all winter. I notice an opening on the left bank. I turn off the machine and scramble up the bank to the woods. It's a trail. The old trail to the Sheenjek cabin. I walk ahead, clearing out a few tree limbs, branches and small blowdowns. Considering how long it's been since it was last traveled, this section of trail seems to be in surprisingly good shape. I consider going back to get the sled and see how far I can get on it. But looking up ahead, I see a large tree spanning the trail a couple feet off the ground. It looks like another one is beyond it. There's an axe in the toboggan and I think on it for a minute. But I haven't discussed it with Jim, I'm a long ways from the cabin with his equipment, and I've other things to do. I walk back to the machine and turn around. In just a few hours, I've had enough excitement for a week!

A picture I'll remember

I'm back at the cabin. It's a nice, quiet evening, dead calm with cooling temperatures. I get the fire roaring in the barrel stove, put away the gear, and hang the three lynx up outside the cabin. I take advantage of the remaining daylight and cut some firewood along the trail a short ways from the cabin yard, hauling it to the cabin in the toboggan. Just before dark I call Jim on the satellite phone he's left with me. We'd planned for a call to check in and make sure there wasn't anything else he would need to bring from town on his trip back tomorrow. Other than a resupply of NyQuill for my nagging cold, I think we're in good shape. Jim shares his news with me first. On his way to Fort Yukon, he picked up a wolverine! It was caught in a lynx snare at the same spot where we'd caught the lynx triple on our way up the other day. The snare was equipped with a kill spring, and fortunately it tightened down and dispatched the animal before it could chew the cable apart and escape, as they're apt to do.

It's hard to hide the enthusiasm in my voice when I mention that I picked up three lynx on the trap line. He sounds as surprised as me. It's quite a catch on a two day check of a relatively short line. Jim says the cold weather is indeed on the way, but he should make it back up tomorrow without any trouble. He says he left me a message on Trapline Chatter, so I'd better tune in to KJNP around 9 P.M.

Trapline Chatter

I cook up some burgers, veggies and lynx meat. We'd saved the meat from the last lynx to supplement our groceries. Cooked very simply in a covered pot on the stove with some onions and a little seasoning, I'm pleasantly surprised by how delicious it turns out to be. With a full stomach and a tired, worn out body, I sit back at the table and reflect on the day. I have about two hours until Trapline Chatter comes on.

Trapline Chatter is a unique radio program with a storied background. Its sponsor station, KJNP, is an AM gospel station in North Pole, on the outskirts of Fairbanks. One winter in the mid 1960's, traveling missionary Don Nelson was weathered out in Fairbanks and had no way of getting word to his remote home village that he wouldn't make it home that night. He appealed to the local radio station to broadcast a message that he'd be delayed, allaying any concerns for his well being by the folks back home.

A few years later, Nelson started KJNP, and Trapline Chatter became a nightly feature. In those days it wasn't just trappers who were out of contact with the outside world. Most remote villages didn't have phone service, so village to village communication was a challenge, and messages often took days or weeks to be delivered.

Trapline Chatter quickly became a daily message service for those wanting to contact anyone in remote Alaska who was otherwise out of reach. From birth announcements to emergencies to visit details and important supply deliveries, the service was widely popular and almost indispensable.

By the mid 1980's, nearly a hundred messages were read on Trapline Chatter each night. Even for the trapper or villager who had no messages coming to them, hearing other folks' messages provided a source of entertainment on those quiet, lonely, dark nights, and a sense of community.

Today, modern technology has reached all the villages – all have phone lines and internet connections. Most trappers living in remote cabins have either a satellite phone or In-Reach satellite messenger, allowing for almost instant contact with the outside world for news and emergencies. Trapline Chatter still airs each night in the winter time, but the messages these days are few and far between.

I'd first heard of Trapline Chatter while watching the 1993 National Geographic documentary "Braving Alaska" featuring Heimo Korth and other remote trappers. In it was an evening scene showing Heimo and his wife Edna sitting by the radio listening to the Trapline Chatter messages. In more recent years, "The Last Alaskans" showed the Korths, the Seldens, the Lewis family and Bob Harte listening to Trapline Chatter from each of their cabins, separated by vast stretches of wilderness. Though it doesn't air until 9 P.M., a full five or six hours after dark and dinner in a trap line cabin, staying up and listening to Trapline Chatter has been a time honored tradition among bush trappers.

Most every night we've been here, Jim and I have tuned in to KJNP to listen for Trapline Chatter messages. The first night we heard a message for Marty Meierotto from his wife and daughter.

Marty is one of the few trappers who continues to trap essentially full time in the bush during the winter months. He spent his career as a smoke jumper and pilot with the Alaska Fire Service in summer and trapper in winter. He maintains an airplane that he uses to get to and from his trap lines. Marty was featured on the cover of Field & Stream magazine about ten years back, accompanied by the title: "The Ultimate Survivor – Life in the Wild with Alaska's Toughest Trapper". For almost a decade he starred in the History Channel's hit TV show "Mountain Men", bringing Alaska wilderness trapping to living rooms worldwide. Jim tells me Marty has an In-Reach these days, but his wife Dominique regularly calls in Trapline Chatter messages. Like us, I'm guessing Marty's nostalgic.

Surprisingly for me, there were no messages on Trapline Chatter a couple of the nights we listened in. It's February, and with so little need for the message service nowadays and many trappers back home and finished for the season, I guess it makes sense. A couple of nights we were unable to get adequate radio signal to hear KJNP. With such clear wintertime air, tuning in to a Fairbanks station would seem pretty easy. Then again, we're shrouded by tall spruces and nearly 200 miles from the station. I'm not sure the reasoning, but stations from all over the state and Canada seem to come and go here with no discernable pattern.

The antenna feeding the old school manual dial AM/FM radio in Jim's cabin is pretty simple. It's a wire attached to a long pole leaning against the cabin roof. Moving it up, down, back, forth and all around doesn't seem to do much, until it does. I have one task between now and 9 P.M.: get a clear enough signal to hear Jim's Trapline Chatter message. I adjust the antenna, run inside, tune around 1170, run back out, and repeat. All to no avail.

It's getting close to 9 and I'm kind of frustrated. From afar I've heard and seen trappers listening to this storied program, and even dreamed about someday sitting in a cabin listening in for a message of my own. Now I'm about to get one and I may not even get to hear it! I've just about given up by 9, but as I twirl the dial back and forth I suddenly hear what appears to be a person reading from the Bible. It's KJNP. It fades in and out, but I can hear it! Now if it just holds for a few more minutes.

Trapline Chatter is on. There's only one message tonight. *"To Jeremiah on the Sheenjek, from Jim Firmin in Fort Yukon. Made it to Fort Yukon, heading back tomorrow. If Bill stops by, give him that box of old books."* A few minutes later, the message is replayed. It's full of static and fades in and out, but I've managed to make a recording of it with my phone. Awesome! Jim hadn't told me the nature of the message, but it's a good one. It's an inside joke, a bit of dry humor. Nobody is stopping by out here. The Bill he's referring to is Bill Russell, the old trapper who lived up the Sheenjek from Jim and Joe's upper cabin. When Bill up and left many years ago, a pile of stuff remained in his cabin. I think Jim and Joe would go over there and grab a few books or magazines when they ran out of reading material. Or, Jim's message might have been referring to our mutual interest in old books and area history. Either way, it's a good one. I have a laugh, stoke up the wood stove, and get to bed.

Wolverine

I've slept in. The cold I'd picked up early in the trip is still hanging on, and I probably needed the rest. I'd left the wood stove damper a bit more open than usual overnight, hoping to keep the cabin warmer. There's always a risk the fire goes out, but a cooling cabin tends to wake me up before that becomes a problem. Sometime in the night I'd stoked it again, and it stayed warm into the morning. I wake and it's almost light already. The thermometer says its 30 below zero outside. Turns out that cold weather they were calling for is here. I turn on the radio and wolf down some breakfast. The forecast is calling for a high of 20 below today, so I'd better dress warm.

Bundled up, I stoke and choke the stove and step outside. It is cold. The Tundra takes a long time to start, and doesn't seem to be very happy until it gets good and warm. For a machine otherwise designed for the conditions of an Alaska trap line, I'm surprised at how poorly these 550 fan Tundras start in cold weather. I use two in Maine that act the same way. I get loaded and head out to the river. Today I check the river-bend cutoff trail and Curtis Slough. It's clear and cold out on the open river, and I'm excited and convinced it's going to be a good day. I cross and climb the opposite bank and head back into the woods.

If yesterday was a lucky day, today will prove to be the opposite, with enough misses and close calls to make the most seasoned trapper hang his head. When we'd opened the cutoff trail, the snow showed very few furbearers had been in the area over the past few weeks, and accordingly, we'd set few traps. But they're here now. A short ways in I spot a fresh set of lynx tracks crossing our trail at the top of a cut bank. I follow the tracks into the woods a ways and set a snare. Down the cut bank, I quickly encounter a fresh set of wolverine tracks. Wolverine! I've always dreamed of catching a wolverine, and have set a number of traps specifically for them since the beginning of the trip, so to see a fresh set of tracks on our trail is exciting. But it's not so exciting to watch it walk past two of our sets. These were lynx sets, with rub lure smeared to a tree, so it's not unreasonable to expect a wolverine to pass them by. For a time I see drag marks in the fresh snow beside the wolverine tracks. It's carrying something. The tracks lead to a hollow spot at the base of a clump of brush. It looks like the wolverine cached something in the snow and brush here. I find a suitable spot nearby and make a cubby set baited with fish, hoping it returns.

I finish out the short cutoff trail and get back on the Porcupine. The sun is up. It's cold but I'm not. I'm dressed warm, and despite experiencing the coldest temperatures since I've been here my body seems to be handling the cold much better than I'd expected. I look across the river at the surrounding trees, and the sun reflecting off the snow at low angles. It's hard to describe how beautiful everything looks this morning. It must be the cold air, holding less moisture and reflecting more light. As good friend and Alaska trapper Josh Fischer once told me, it's like seeing everything in high definition. Another level.

I ride up river and enter Curtis Slough, and it's immediately apparent there's been a lot of activity here over the past few days. At least three sets of fresh lynx tracks crossed the slough and investigated our sets. One walked around one of our snares. Another walked right up to a snare, evidently noticed it and got shy, backed out and turned around. A third lynx walked into a set that I'd forgotten Jim had pulled the trap from to set it elsewhere. It had come to the cubby, investigated it, and stepped exactly where the pan of the trap would have been – if it were still there!

Fresh wolverine tracks suddenly enter the slough, and I follow along intently for a quarter mile. The tracks and I are both heading to where I'd caught that first lynx and also had a 330 set for wolverine. This is exciting stuff! I look behind me and notice a thick trail of vapor from the snowmobile exhaust. This must be that ice fog Alaska trappers have told me about in the past, a reminder of how cold it is. The wolverine tracks weave back and forth from shore to shore - apparently it was looking for food. This is good – better chance it stumbled into one of our sets. The wolverine tracks go right past one of the sets, but go directly into the next. I'm at the spot where we'd made a foothold set and 330 box set targeting wolverine. The tracks follow our trail into the brush, but the wolverine walked around the lynx snare we'd set in the trail. It then went straight to the baited cubby set in the willows and stole the bait without stepping on the trap. Finally, I look over to see the 330 on the ground, set off a few feet from the box. Somehow the wolverine, while investigating the set, caused the trap to fire without getting caught. Unbelievable.

It's a bittersweet afternoon, the disappointment of so many missed close calls mixed with the incredible beauty all around me and the enjoyment of a quiet, crystal clear day in solitude. The ride on the river back to the cabin is a bit chilly, but not too bad. I'm back to the cabin about a half hour after Jim's arrival from Fort Yukon. He brought the wolverine with him, the first one I get to see and handle in person. It's quite a beast. If I remember right it weighs about 38 pounds. It's a massive ball of muscle and fur, with a combination of dark brown guard hairs and underfur and a distinctive golden colored strip of fur on each side running from the midsection to the base of the tail. I've heard other trappers call this the 'crown', and its size, color and distinctiveness varies by animal. More light colored fur gathers in small patches in a mottled configuration around the throat. I see a similar pattern in the furs of marten I trap back home.

Wolverine!

The wolverine has always been a fascinating animal to me, for probably an extreme version of the same reason I love marten. They require wild places to survive, and if you're in wolverine habitat, you're likely far from civilization, in a harsh environment only the tough, strong-willed and stubborn thrive. The wolverine has a reputation for being particularly tough, from fighting off packs of wolves to defend its food to being able to crush bones and tear into frozen hide and flesh of moose and caribou. The wolverine isn't really a predator, though. He's primarily a scavenger, living near ample sources of dead animals and ranging far and wide when needed. Wolverines tend to be particularly abundant in places where both wolves and their prey – moose and caribou – thrive, because these areas provide ample opportunity to scavenge on dead carcasses. One thing is for certain, wolverines do not seem to thrive around civilization. Perhaps it's the noise and activity of humans, the lack of excess large game, or, more likely, the simple coincidence that most humans don't thrive in extremely cold and remote climates, while wolverines require them. The vast forests of Alaska and northern Canada harbor large, healthy populations of wolverines, as do the Nordic countries of mainland Europe, the vast wilderness areas of Russia, and parts of China and Mongolia. While far less common, wolverines also extend into the high alpine country and wilderness areas of the Lower 48. Small breeding populations are believed to occur in Oregon, Washington, Idaho, Montana and Wyoming. It is believed that historic overharvest and other human related impacts caused these populations to diminish throughout much of their range in the Lower 48, and wolverines are beginning to recolonize these areas in modern times, with recent sightings occurring in California and Colorado.

Wolverine populations throughout most of Alaska and Canada appear to be very healthy these days. The relatively high trapping pressure in the early days probably kept their numbers down a bit, and Jim remembers that catching one or two a year was pretty typical. These days, with the same amount of effort, catching four or five in a season is common. The fur is very valuable, with pelts averaging in the $300-400 range. Most of these remain in the state and are sold to native or traditional artisans who use the fur for parka ruffs (where it uniquely resists the buildup of frost) and other clothing items.

We admire the wolverine, take pictures of each other holding it up in the cabin yard, and talk about how Jim found it dead in one of the snares we'd set down river. To me, one of the most exciting things about this trip is the opportunity to catch a wolverine, and now I get to see one up close. It's believed that wolverines were historically found in my home state of Maine, although I've been able to find little evidence to back these claims. If so, they were likely present in the times when vast herds of woodland caribou roamed the state and were chased by packs of wolves. It was a different world back then. More like this place is today. I did trap for wolverine once. That is, I set one trap on a set of what I was quite sure were wolverine tracks while marten trapping in the vast wilderness of the Beartooth Mountains of Montana. The Big Sky state is the only place left in the Lower 48 that allows wolverine trapping, but it's on a very restricted basis. When I trapped there, the statewide quota for wolverine was three animals. When I made the set, I recalled seeing what I was pretty certain was a wolverine in the next drainage over while hiking at timberline the previous summer. But that was many years ago, and the animal that had left the tracks and inspired me to make the set didn't return that season.

In passing, Jim offers me this wolverine. It's a particularly generous gesture, considering that at its size and pelt quality, he could probably sell this one for close to $500. I can't accept. After all of the costs he's incurred to take me along, I can't take this kind of money from his pocket. Plus, he made the sets, and he found it in the trap. It's his wolverine. I have traps out, and pretty high hopes that I'll pick up one of my own in the coming days. If I don't, that's okay too. This trip is about more than wolverine.

Cold

The cold snap has arrived. When we initially planned this trip, the weather had been an important factor in the decision-making process. When the temperature drops below minus 40 degrees, even the toughest trappers think twice about going out to check traps. When it drops closer to minus 50, things get real serious. Machines don't start, and they don't run all that well either. Metal becomes brittle. Breakdowns are less inconvenience and more serious threat to survival. Frostbite happens. Cold air burns the lungs. A cold body can't move enough to warm back up. At these temperatures, any mistake, mishap or bad luck can kill you. And plus, the animals hunker down too. In most cases, running the trap line in these conditions is risky and can be a bit of a waste of time. We'd chosen February for my visit to avoid one of those cold snaps that more commonly occur in December and January. Being stuck in a cabin for a week, waiting for the weather to warm up enough to go trapping could really put a damper on things.

Now that Jim's back and all our lines are out, he plans to stay at the cabin while I run the lines for the next few days. But Mother Nature's having her say as well. It's 35 below when daylight comes, and the snowmachine won't start. After several attempts, Jim suggests we wait for things to warm up. I take the chainsaw down the trail a short ways in the timber and cut some firewood while waiting for the sun to rise and bring some warmth to the cabin yard. An hour later, it's up to minus 20-25 and the machine starts. Good!

I'm off through the woods, down the river and to the backwater slough "Gy-Roo". It's the first check on the line we set up here a couple days ago. Given the relatively numerous lynx and hare tracks we'd seen here before, I'm pretty optimistic. But I needn't be. No trap is sprung, no snare fired. In the entire circuit I don't see a single fresh lynx or wolverine track in the snow. It's dead. Is the cold weather keeping animals from moving? Did the lynx that left tracks here earlier take up and leave the country? I don't know, but it's a discouraging ride back to the cabin. The only good news I can come up with is that I've handled the cold weather surprisingly well today. I tell myself I must be getting used to it!

It's cold!

It's Thursday, February 13, and the thermometer reads 45 degrees below zero. The cold is here in full force, with no sign of letting up soon. All of our lines are set out, all have been recently checked, and the fur isn't moving much with the cold. With just a few days left of my time here, it's too late to justify cutting more trail and setting more traps. The cold weather is hard on equipment, and the machines are owned by my host, not me. If I break something, he's stuck having to fix it. Despite my strong desire to get out and do something, I agree with Jim that it's better to stay at the cabin today.

It's a slow day. I try to pass the time, but I'm restless. You can only drink so much coffee and tea, tell so many stories, sit for so long. I watch the thermometer, but it moves little. I do a bit of reading. Jim is tinkering around the cabin, cleaning and organizing, rearranging small items here and there. He's getting ready to skin the wolverine. Finally, bored out of my mind, I bundle up and go out for a walk. The blanket of cold air outside is a pretty powerful force. I walk the trail from the cabin at a brisk pace, hoping to generate body heat and get warmer, but the internal furnace takes a lot longer than normal to get up to temperature. My rubber boots make a deafeningly loud, squeaky creaking noise each time they make contact with the hard snow on the trail. I stop for a second, and everything is dead silent.

I make the trek across the wide expanse of the Porcupine and climb the steep bank on the other side, continuing along an open flat with patches of brush. I follow the trail for a while longer, reaching the change in terrain where I'd set a lynx snare and made a cubby set for wolverine the other day. These are untouched, and I haven't seen a single fresh track of any kind on my travels. I return to the high bank of the river. I stop in the open and look around. The sun is low in the horizon, but at its high point for the day. It shines on the vast expanse of spruce trees that line the river and reflects off the snow. I'm finally warm, and I take a seat in the snow at the top of the bank. Everything is bright, sunny, crystal clear and dead calm. I hear a bird call, and a few hundred yards upstream, a raven is on the move. All is silent again. No motors, no voices, no people, anywhere near here. I think I could get used to this.

Back near the cabin I set a few rabbit snares on some trails close by. There are a fair number of their tracks around, though Jim says they are on the down swing. Snaring rabbits is one of the activities I wanted to make sure I did while up here. It's another thing that isn't legal in Maine, though my grandparents and others of their generation often talked of snaring rabbits for food when times were tough. It's legal and commonplace in the Alaska bush, and some years can be an important source of food for trappers and their families. Since I've been up here, though, chasing lynx, wolverines and wolves has made it easy to forget about rabbits. I have plenty of time to get at it today, though, and I pick out a few of the better looking trails and set snares until it's dark.

Neighbors in the Bush

Back into what's become our regular routine, Jim and I sit at the table after supper and talk trapping. Our conversation turns to area trappers, past and present. Though I've never met them, the stories I hear of the different characters who have roamed this area in the recent past paint a good picture.

Our closest neighbors here, Tyler and Ashley Selden, are unreachable up the Sheenjek, unless one chartered a plane. If we traveled up the Porcupine, it would take a day or two of steady driving, and lots of extra snowmachine gas, to reach the next active trapline, manned by Charlie Jagow. An ambitious young man in his early twenties, Charlie is unique to most young people these days in that he grew up out here, along with his sister and their parents, in a small cabin on the Porcupine that his father built. The son of a successful corporate lawyer in New York City, Paul Jagow came here to trap in the late 1970's. He lived alone in a small sod hut he'd built, trapping and living an isolated existence from freezeup to breakup each year. Eventually he met Dawn, another New Yorker, in Fairbanks, and they began spending their summers in town and winters on the 'line. Now retired, Paul and Dawn live in Fairbanks, but spend time out here most winters. Charlie has taken over his father's trap lines, and expanded beyond their former boundaries, using a small bush plane to access more ground in a season than his father could have dreamed of. Charlie was featured on the TV show "The Last Alaskans". His trapping area lies within the Arctic National Wildlife Refuge, where permanent human occupation has been banned by the Federal Government. Having been established there prior to the formation of the Refuge, Paul and his children, along with about half a dozen other families, are the only people permitted to remain there. Charlie is the youngest permit holder, and may truly be the last occupant of this vast wilderness country. He built a new log cabin a couple years back, and has made impressive catches of fur in his effort to sustain a living here. Charlie also earns income guiding hunters here in the fall. Smart, hard working and wise beyond his years, the young man has a bright future ahead of him.

Just over the hill from Charlie (okay, more like 30 or 40 miles) sits an unoccupied cabin on the bank of the Coleen River. Bob Harte built this one, after taking over the abandoned country where crusty old prospector and trapper Ed Owens had once lived. Like most, Owens came to Alaska from the states. He was a prospector first and foremost, and eternally optimistic he'd someday discover a rich find. Owens trapped some, mostly to provide the limited amount of income he needed to survive. He married a native woman from village of Old Crow, further up the Porcupine River in Canada. They raised two daughters on the Coleen, but Ed was a rough man, apparently hard to live with. One year his wife and daughters took off down the Porcupine, leaving Ed alone to live out the rest of his days.

In his declining years, Owens sold his cabin and trap line to Charlie Wolf, an Ohio-born man who had retired from military service in Alaska. Rather than move to town he moved further up river and continued prospecting, to a limited degree, despite being crippled by old age. He was found dead in his cabin yard one winter at age 86. Wolf trapped out of Ed's old cabin for about a decade, but lost interest. He became well known for his long canoe voyages across Canada and Alaska, spending months at a time traveling rivers despite his advancing age. In the early 1970's a young Tom McGuire joined Charlie on a canoe trip from the headwaters of the Yukon River nearly to its mouth, and documented it in his book "99 Days on the Yukon".

Not long after Charlie Wolf abandoned the old Owens trap line on the Coleen, another young adventurer arrived. New Jersey-born Bob Harte had caught the wilderness bug after spending some time in southeast Alaska. Jim Firmin remembers meeting Bob when he first arrived in Fort Yukon, camped out on a gravel bar, looking for a place to trap in the wilderness. It was around 1974. In Bob's ex-wife Nancy Becker's 2020 book "Trapline Chatter: Life and Love with 'Last Alaskan' Bob Harte", she quotes from Bob's journal, "*I hitchhiked to Eagle and asked about the trapping. Then I hitchhiked to Circle and asked about the trapping. Next, I got in a canoe and canoed down river to Fort Yukon. That was deep interior and top fur country in the state of Alaska. That caught my eye.*"

Bob Harte was built for this place. After an unsuccessful winter trapping from a cabin he'd built on the Christian River, he heard about Ed Owens' territory, and learned that nobody was trapping there. Bob soon made his way up the Porcupine and the Coleen, and built a cabin a short ways from Ed's old place, now abandoned and fading with time. Bob was to live and trap here for the next forty years. Like his 'neighbors', he starred in "The Last Alaskans" and captured the heart and soul of audiences worldwide. To see someone with so much emotion and love for the area, trapping, and living in this wilderness environment on the screen was pretty moving. It was a lonely, regretful, grateful and reminiscent Bob Harte who passed away from a long illness during the filming of the show. Prior to his passing, Bob, who felt a strong desire to ensure his work here wasn't destined to fade from existence, passed his trap lines on to Charlie Jagow, who continues to run them today.

The only other trapper up the Coleen might be the most famous one in America, though you'd never know it from talking with him. Heimo Korth is the closest thing to a modern day version of the old wilderness trappers as it gets. He left his home town in Wisconsin in 1975, both seeking wilderness and fleeing a rough family life. Heimo got his start working for a hunting guide in the Brooks Range. The eager greenhorn made a lot of mistakes and had some close calls early on, but he was determined to stick it out and become a wilderness trapper. After spending time trapping on Beaver Creek and the Chandalar River, Heimo found himself living and trapping on the upper Coleen in 1978. He and his wife Edna, a native from the St. Lawrence Island village of Savoonga, have lived a subsistence lifestyle there for more than 40 years, raising three daughters in the process.

Most years the Korths would live in one of three cabins they'd built in the Coleen River country for all but a month and a half in the summer, where they'd visit Fort Yukon to purchase supplies, catch up with friends and earn a little income. In more recent years their children have settled in Fairbanks and grandkids are a major draw, bringing them out of the bush a bit longer each year. But come fall, they're back up north preparing for the long winter and trapping season. Jim knows Heimo well. Both being members of the shrinking fraternity of trappers in the area, they spend a great deal of time swapping stories and catching up on Heimo's trips to Fort Yukon and Fairbanks.

Despite living such an isolated lifestyle, Heimo is as friendly and outgoing as they come. He's been featured in multiple documentaries, "The Last Alaskans", and "The Final Frontiersman", a book about his life story written by his cousin, James Campbell. Even in his 60's Heimo runs long trap lines and puts up a good pile of fur most years. He's fairly determined to continue living this lifestyle for as long as his body allows.

Those are the trappers who have roamed the area in recent years, and Jim tells various stories about one or the other when some topic of conversation triggers a memory. But there's one old Fort Yukon trapper he speaks of with particular fondness – Fred Thomas. Probably the most accomplished lynx trapper of his time, Fred was a mentor to guys like Jim and Heimo. He was born in May 1919, and shortly afterward, his mother and father headed on their annual journey up the Black River to trap.

Jacob Thomas, Fred's father, was born in Wisconsin sometime around 1880 and came to Alaska during the Gold Rush. Mining didn't pan out for him, but he fell in love with the country and its people. For fifteen or twenty years, Thomas worked on the steamboats freighting supplies up and down the Yukon, and earned the name "Tommy the Mate".

The Thomas family would boat up the Black River far above Chalkyitsik. Early on, Thomas trapped around the Salmon Village area and later moved upstream to the Grayling Fork. After trapping all winter, the family would return to Fort Yukon around the first of June. They would sell fur, secure an outfit for the following year and take care of other business, and head back up the Porcupine and the Black in late July or early August. The journey was more than 200 miles by boat, and would often take about a month.

Fred was the oldest in a big family. After his father died he took over as head of the family, learning to trap while teaching and guiding his younger brothers, who referred to him as 'The Captain'. The brothers trapped together for a long time, even after Fred was married and had a child of his own. They covered a vast territory and caught incredible numbers of fur. Fred, his brother and his son caught 315 lynx one season, and the cats averaged around $350 apiece! Fred told his brother Albert, "*When you say...the good old days....it's right now!*"

Fred's long trap lines up the Black River took a pause when his kids reached school age, and he and his wife Charlotte moved to Fort Yukon and Fred took a job at the Air Force Base. Upon retirement in 1976 he resumed trapping full time. In his essay "Up the Black to Chalkyitsik", from the book "Balancing Acts", Edward Hoagland paints a picture of Fred in his post-retirement years while joining him on a river trip from Fort Yukon one fall.

Even as an old man Fred had his wits about him, and being one of the last long line trappers around town, Jim often visited him with questions or to gain a better historical perspective on things. Fred was an honest man who worked hard for everything he had and never asked for a handout from anyone. Even in his eighties he was running about 100 miles of line from Fort Yukon, and he trapped until three years before he died in 2018, at age 98.

Back on the Line

It's Friday, February 14th, and -50 degrees right on the nose. The thought of loafing around the cabin for another full day is looming over me like a dark cloud. Jim can sense this, and at breakfast time he suggests we try preheating the Tundra when daylight comes. If it starts, I can take it and run some line today. In the interim, I take the pot of water we keep on the stove for tea, and head outside for an experiment. No doubt you've heard of water turning to steam at 50 below. Having never seen it in person, I have to give it a shot. With a swing of the pot, I launch the hot water into the air, and it instantly dissipates in a cloud of steam. Check that one off the list.

With a collection of tarps, blankets and wooden poles we improvise a mini tent over the cab of the snowmachine to insulate it from the surrounding air. We set up a single burner camp stove, with a stovepipe elbow and a short length of pipe to direct heat to the machine's engine compartment.

The warmup process is painstakingly slow at 50 below. I take the thermometer from the cabin wall and place it under the tarp so I can check the temperature every ten minutes or so. It barely moves.

Preheating the snowmachine

Beside me and outside of the tarp-blanket shelter, the machine's foam seat is hard as a rock. After a while, Jim takes hold of the pull starter and leans back to see how easily the engine will turn over.

Not easy. He says it's counterproductive to pull it at these temperatures because it causes the super cold air to be sucked into the engine, and prolongs the whole process. So we wait.

By 11 A.M. the preheating has done its job, and the Tundra turns over, catches and sputters until it starts. I make a couple of last minute preparations and take off down the trail to Snake Lake. For all of the preparation in getting going, it's a pretty short line to run, and the route down the lake and through the woods, ending at the wolverine set on the creek, is fairly uneventful. Nothing is in our traps, though I notice three fresh sets of lynx tracks, one of whose owner walked by a couple of sets and knocked down one of our

Lynx tracks on our trail

trail snares. I spot a wolverine track not far from where I'd made the pen set for marten, and make a similar set with a larger trap for wolverine. A couple of wolves have crossed Snake Lake, but they didn't stick around very long and we have no wolf sets there. I return to the cabin with little to share, and daylight to spare.

Since I'm dressed and the machine is warmed up, I take the

opportunity to cut some ice from the river to add to our drinking water supply. Water is critical for survival, and most who live in remote, 'dry' cabins chip a hole in the ice to dip water from the river for drinking and cabin use. Though clean snow is abundant all around, it isn't practical to melt snow for water due to the sheer volume of snow required to get a tiny bit of water. Using ice is another way. Jim first learned of this from Jimmy Ward when he stayed with him at Shuman House in the '70's. You find a spot on the river where big cakes of ice jammed up during the freezing process the previous fall. One of these places exists not far from Jim's cabin, in a riffle area of the Porcupine, and cakes of ice several inches thick jut up from the otherwise smooth surface of surrounding river ice and snow. A clean axe and a toboggan are all that are needed, and the cakes are chopped off at their base and tossed in the sled. Larger pieces are desired, as they make for less handling. Once hauled back to the cabin yard, they are stacked together and covered with a piece of canvas to keep the birds from messing on them. When the cabin water gets low, you take one of the galvanized pails that always sits near or on the wood stove, and a kitchen knife out to the stack. A few jabs with the kitchen knife easily break off smaller ice chunks to fill the pail and bring to the warm cabin for melting. Simple as that. Though it's a big river, there's no pollution here, nothing to dirty the water or make it unsuitable for drinking. For a wilderness trapper, that's a valuable resource in itself.

It's morning again and not much warmer than yesterday – 45 below. I only have three days left here, one more run through each of the lines. After discussing with Jim, I decide to wait one more day to check the line on Curtis Slough for the last time. It's here I have the highest hopes to catch a wolverine, and an extra day might make the difference. I stay in the cabin and do some writing for a couple of hours, jotting down thoughts and ideas, and portions of what's to become this whole story. I've kept a daily journal thus far, but haven't taken the time to go into any topic at length. This writing gives me a sense of accomplishment despite being cooped up. The sun is low but bright, and it warms to minus 30 by mid day. I help Jim with some camp chores, and it's back to minus 40 by the end of the day. The forecast is calling for warmer weather in the coming days.

It's cold in the cabin. The air setting was a bit tight on the stove overnight, a setting that prevents the fire from burning out, but doesn't allow it to put out near as much heat. The warming predicted in last night's weather forecast hasn't made its way here yet. It's 48 below zero outside, and below freezing here in the cabin. Despite wearing all my long underwear, multiple layers of wool socks, several thermal and fleece upper layers and a knit cap on my head, while tucked into two layers of sleeping bags, I'm still a bit cold. I pick up the Nalgene bottle from the floor near my cot to get a drink. The water in it is frozen. We get the fire blazing and stand near the stove for warmth. I have to laugh as I try to put my contact lenses in. The contacts are frozen into solid blocks of ice in the case I'd left on the table. I remember reading Evelyn Berglund Shore's stories about water freezing on the stove top in her and Bill Grinnell's trap line cabins. The idea seemed outrageous to me at the time, but now it seems like less of a big deal. It's certainly uncomfortable, which I'm even more reminded of upon visiting the outhouse, but it's manageable, and with shelter and a good fire, you quickly warm back up.

I put on every piece of clothing I've brought with me and head out to warm the snowmachine. I made a rookie mistake by leaving my boots on the floor overnight, realizing Jim's typical placement of boots on a shelf near the cabin's ceiling is probably based on experience. I get the warming apparatus together and the stove running, and stamp around the cabin yard to get warm. It takes a while, probably an hour, to get the machine where it will start. By then I'm ready, and get going on the long trip upriver to Curtis Slough.

There's lots of activity evident in the snow since the last time I was here, just prior to the big cold snap. The wolves have been back. Their massive tracks traverse the snow-covered ice, on and off my snowmachine trail, and exploring various features along the banks. The wolf trails parallel mine for several miles. I reach the area where Jim and I set four wolf snares back in the brush where we'd seen their activity more than a week ago and assumed there'd been a kill. Based on the tracks, they milled around this area for a while, but only one track went into the brush where our snares were set, and it walked neatly around a snare set in one of the trails. I take pictures of the wolf tracks and wolf droppings next to my mittens for size reference. They're absolutely massive, almost unbelievably large for someone not too familiar with wolf tracks. I continue up the slough, and the wolf tracks eventually leave my trail.

It's sunny out, cold and clear. I'm a bit cold, but the wolf activity got my blood pumping and I'm excited for what might be ahead. Fresh lynx tracks cross the slough in several places, and a fresh set of wolverine tracks has traversed the same area as last week. "*They've been back*," I tell myself, "*This could be really good.*" I'm getting closer to the area where I'd missed the wolverine earlier. The next spot is one of our typical setups, with a couple of trail snares next to a foothold cubby set for lynx, a short ways up the bank from the river in a willow patch. There's evidence of lots of activity here, both lynx and wolverine tracks, so much so that I can't interpret it too well. I walk into the woods to check the traps. Almost instantly I see a lynx dead in a snare uphill from me. Finally a catch, after a brutally slow several days! But when I approach the set to remove the cat, something's wrong. It's been eaten, badly. An entire side of the lynx's body has been torn open and devoured, completely ruining the fur. *So that's where the wolverine tracks come in.* It gets worse when I look to the cubby set just a few feet above here. The trap, a #4 Bridger, is sprung. I look closer. Long strands of black hair protrude

The wolverine got to this lynx before I did

from between the trap's two closed jaws. Wolverine.

I remake the sets and bring the torn up lynx carcass out to the toboggan. I'll bring it back. Jim might get a few bucks for the skull, and we can use the remainder of the carcass for bait. It's discouraging. I can't seem to wrap my head around how I lost that wolverine, but upon further reflection, the long guard hairs are probably from its rear end, and it probably sat on the trap while in the process of destroying the lynx I'd caught. Only having some of

Wolverine hair in the trap

its hair gripped in the trap, the wolverine easily pulled out.

I'm now discouraged about the next set, even though it's the place that holds the best chance of catching the wolverine on this slough, with a baited cubby guarded with a #4 double long spring trap and a 330 box set. I wonder if the experience at the last set will keep the predator from visiting others, but as I get closer, I notice the same set of tracks in the snow headed in that direction. I enter the woods, following the tracks, and lay eyes on the greatest disappointment of my short wolverine trapping career. I caught a wolverine. But I didn't hold him. Most Alaska trappers will tell you that it isn't super hard to catch a wolverine, but keeping one caught can be near impossible at times. Such a ferocious creature doesn't take well to being restrained, and unlike a lynx, they attempt to destroy and tear up everything within reach. This wolverine had torn apart the cubby and wrapped itself around the clump of willows the trap was chained to. At some point it achieved just the right force at just the right angle, and pulled free from the trap, with a couple of small spots of blood adding evidence of the struggle. Just as easily as it had approached the set, the tracks in the snow show the wolverine walking away and continuing up the slough. In utter disbelief, and with a few choice words, I remake the set and move on. I've officially experienced the greatest letdown of my trapping life.

In the second to last stop on the slough there's a live lynx in a foothold trap, providing a nice distraction from the disbelief I'm in after losing the wolverine. It's a pretty lynx, and the frost on its guard hairs shimmers in the low midday sun. I take a few pictures and enjoy the moment. Despite the letdowns, it's been one heck of an experience here, and I don't intend to waste it. I dispatch the lynx and take my time visiting the last set. The ride back down river is filled with thoughts as I try to process the ups and downs of the day, and the trip. I also have thoughts about the future. Jim will pull these sets for the season in a week or two, but I've made my last trip upriver. I wonder when I'll be back, or if I'll be back.

The warm weather comes. It's 38 below the next morning and projected to warm to -15 by day's end. It's funny how the human body adapts to its surroundings. This temperature would have felt almost unbearable for me a couple weeks ago. Today it seems relatively mild. And as I run the lines, I've begun to feel somewhat at home here. I check Gy-Roo and the surrounding spur trails from the cabin one last time. Not a single animal, and almost no fresh tracks. The extended cold snap apparently slowed animal movement to a halt. It will pick up again next week, I figure. I leave the sets in for Jim to check when he returns, and we begin to pack and prepare for the trip to Fort Yukon.

It's no wolverine, but I'll take it

Returning Home

The small plane picks up speed quickly on the runway, and before I know it, we're in the air. Only two other passengers are with me. We'd waited for a few minutes before taking off for one last passenger who wasn't showing. The pilot, a clean shaven red haired guy about 30, looked at his list. "We're waiting for a guy from Maine."

"I'm your guy" I told him from the seat a few rows back, pretty certain nobody else was returning to Maine that day. Satisfied, he made some final checks and we were on our way.

When we've gained enough altitude, I glue myself to the window. It's a clear day with excellent visibility and I try to soak in as much of the country as possible. After a couple of weeks seeing it from the ground, I can paint a better picture in my mind of the spruce forests, open lakes and winding sloughs we're flying over. The young lady sitting behind me taps me on the shoulder. She offers to take a picture of me with my phone. It's a kind gesture. Another memory preserved.

The last couple of days have been a drag. Kind of a slow limbo between the wilderness trapline and life back in civilization. We'd come in early to avoid missing today's flight, just in case a breakdown or change in the weather got us delayed. But all went well on the ride home. We even picked up a bonus lynx in one of the sets along the Porcupine a few miles out of town.

First leg of the trip home

Back at Jim's place, crowded in among the other small lots and cabins huddled together in town, I sat there and waited. It was bitter cold outside, with no reason to go out, and dark inside. The wilderness, open spaces and isolation were gone. But so were the comforts of home and conveniences – TV and internet, for instance, to pass the time. I browsed maps, asked about different trappers and their lines, and read everything I could find. We visited the CATG office – Council of Athabascan Tribal Governments –

another agency in the complex mix of federal, state and tribal entities that help run the place. Bruce Thomas, the director of Natural Resources, agreed to come by and tag our lynx pelts so I could ship a few home. We talked about the bush, trapping, and the hunting and fishing issues they'd been dealing with. A pleasant guy, laughing at most anything, he looked at me intently with a questioning eye the few times I spoke. I suppose a guy coming to this isolated area to chase after a few low value fur pelts is a bit of an enigma.

Tommy Ward, grandson of legendary trapper Joe Ward stopped by one afternoon. He'd gone upriver with Jim the previous spring to help work on the cabin for several days. Sitting across the table, he stared at me for long periods of time when either of us spoke. Tommy's father Jimmy was one of the last generation who grew up in the bush, but his son had grown up more anchored to town. He'd had a rough past, riddled with drugs, alcohol and tangles with the law, but now in his later years, didn't seem jaded by any of it. He talked of starting up a guiding business, taking outsiders up river to stay at his cabin, bringing in big money while giving people a taste of the wilderness. Tommy would ask me a challenging question, then watch me with a steady poker face, waiting for my response, seemingly hoping to catch me in an incorrect answer. Eventually he excused himself, got up and left, leaving me unsure whether I'd passed the test.

After shipping furs at the post office, I browsed around the Alaska Commercial Company store on Main Street for gifts to take home for the wife and kids. A pleasant lady who worked the checkout showed me a small display case with some handmade jewelry and a collection of postcards. Bundled up and sweating in my warm clothing, I selected a few things, paid, and headed out to the cooler entryway of the store to wait for Jim. A flyer from CATG announced an upcoming wolf snaring seminar, where free snares would be given to all attendees. It was part of an effort to control predator numbers in a place where most of the residents rely on moose meat to get through the winter. Just a generation ago, the majority of the male population in this area were active trappers or had been on a trapline sometime in their life. Wolf control and food security had taken care of themselves. Times changed.

Leaving the Flats

The ground begins to rise below us. We're leaving the Yukon Flats and approaching the White Mountains. In my daydreaming I wonder if we've flown over the section of Beaver Creek where Charley Mayse had his traplines. Charley was another who lived in that era between the old fur trappers who were scattered throughout the woods and the large scale abandonment of the country today. He'd bought the trapline on Beaver Creek from Dick Morris, an old timer who'd lived alone out there for many years, built an impressive operation, and supported himself solely by catching and selling fur. Mayse moved to Alaska from the Pacific Northwest later in life, seeking the bush lifestyle and fascinated by the history. He spent several seasons out on the Beaver Creek line, about 90 river miles up from the Yukon and the village of Beaver, mostly trapping the old trails on foot or with dogs. He'd catch beavers and muskrats on the creek, lynx in the flats, and marten in the higher ground, presumably, I assume, in some of the foothills I'm flying over now. He called himself an 'escapist', seeking the wilderness to "get out from under the overseer's whip, to be my own man".

Later in life Charley spent most of his time in Fairbanks, researching history, interviewing old timers as part of the Tanana Yukon Historical Society, writing outdoor articles and hanging out with his buddy Sam White, the legendary old bush pilot and game warden.

We fly over the mountains, inching closer to the Tanana Valley and the greater Fairbanks area. This is the last of bush Alaska I'll see in quite a while, I'm sure. But for how long? I'd dreamed of coming to Alaska a couple of decades before, and now that I'm leaving it, the only thing I can seem to think about is how to get back.

It's true that one can drop everything, quit their job and move into the woods, even today. We live in a free society and there's lots of open country out there. But possible and feasible are two different things, and the distinction is at the root of a struggle that now seems to be violently pulling me in two directions.

Back in the heyday of the bush trappers, a hard worker on a productive trapline could make enough money in the winter months to pay for most of a year's living expenses. It was a good run. The world fur market was strong. Demand for fur coats, hats and other items outpaced the supply of wild furs and a ranch fur industry that was only in its infancy. The fur district of New York was bustling, full of garment manufacturers, dealers and exporters of fur items. This economic phenomenon trickled down to the bush villages, where the cold interior Alaska climate produced the fullest and most luxurious furs available. Fur provided an important source of income to families who were transitioning from a nomadic lifestyle to a modern day cash society in a place where there were no jobs. It also fueled the dreams of many young men like Jim and Joe Firmin who moved to the bush to seek out a lifestyle, and found a way to make it pay.

Jim's fur sale receipts, fur updates and flyers date back to the early 1970's, when he sold his first furs out of Fort Yukon. He saved every one. They bear the names of companies that no long exist: H.E. Goldberg & Co. of Seattle, the Seattle Fur Exchange, Western Canadian Raw Fur Auction Sales, Dominion/Soudack Fur Auction Sales and others.

Even in the 1980's the market for Alaskan furs, though well off some of the highs seen in previous decades, was adequate to make a decent living. In 1984 Jim shipped a collection of about 50 pelts, part of a season's catch, consisting mainly of marten and lynx. The marten averaged $48.80 and the lynx $273.94. Along with a couple of mink and a few fox, the total from the Seattle Fur Exchange, after commissions, came out to a little over $4,000. In 2021 dollars, this relatively modest catch equated to more than $10,000. At these numbers, a trapper could work a seasonal job in the summer time and take the winter months off to live in the bush, and could make enough to support a family while living a lifestyle that many of us dream of.

The fur market isn't quite dead today, but it's dangerously close. Fur fell out of fashion in the U.S. long, long ago. Demand for fur persisted in small pockets, like parts of New York City, but was mainly supported by a shift to fur consumption by emerging economies in other countries, like China and South Korea. Increasing production of ranch-raised fur has cut into demand for wild fur over the years. A steady slowing in growth of fur-consuming economies overseas combined with the fall of fur in high fashion circles has made things worse. Despite fur's many qualities – warmth, beauty, durability, sustainability and organic makeup – many major fashion lines have disavowed the use of fur, citing animal welfare concerns. Many people simply don't like the fact that animals are killed for fur. We kill animals every day, directly or indirectly, for the food we eat. Leather, which comes from slaughtered domestic cattle, is everywhere. Furbearing animals are abundant, well managed by wildlife agencies, and can support far greater harvest levels than we see today. Lack of harvest resulting from poor markets has led to overpopulation, disease and animal damage problems throughout North America in recent years. But the stigma behind killing animals for fur continues to drive the market's decline.

A 2021 collection of Alaskan marten pelts sold at auction through Fur Harvesters Auction, Inc., the last remaining wild fur auction company in North America these days, went for around the same $40 level that Jim received in 1984. The increased cost of living over the past four decades means that in real terms, these pelts would need to bring more than $100 each to be worth the same as they were back then. But that's not the half of it. Those lynx pelts that brought a $270 plus average in the '80's would need to be worth more than $700 today. In 2021 they brought around $60. Other common species of Alaskan furs sell for similarly disappointing prices these days.

When looking at things from an economic perspective, it makes sense that most of the bush country is abandoned today. Even those with a strong desire to live of the land can't afford to do it. Most of the few who still do are retired (like Jim) or have good summer jobs and sacrifice a great deal in order to make it work. Being on TV during the recent Alaska reality show craze helped a few, but it was a temporary blip. For more than 150 years, frontiersmen who sought a primitive lifestyle on the edge of the modern world could do so partly by catching and selling fur. Deep down inside, I fear we've reached the end of an era.

Streets lined with houses, stores and parking lots abound below us. We're descending into Fairbanks. I've arranged a pickup from my old friend and Fairbanks resident Josh Fischer. It was Josh who I'd spent those evenings with back at the University of Maine, poring over maps of Alaska and talking dreams of building cabins and cutting trapline trails. We're both many years separated from those dreams, and not much closer to realizing them, if we're honest. But this trip has been motivation, as will my future conversations with Josh. I've gotten a taste of the Alaska bush, and I don't know if I'll be able to shrug it off and move on to other things like I did back in those early years.

After visiting with Josh and his family I'll be headed back to Maine, to a stable full time job that pays a great salary, health insurance, paid time off and a retirement plan. The income supports my family, a wonderful wife and two young boys, with a third to come. It allows for other projects, including a growing beef cattle farm and woodlots managed for sustainable timber harvest, all things I love and enjoy. But it doesn't allow me to spend months alone in the Alaska bush, running trails blazed by the old timers and connecting with a place where a growing part of me feels I belong. I only get a taste.

Books Referenced in this Text

Hunters of the Northern Forest *by* Richard K. Nelson
Frank Yasuda and the Chandalar *by* Ernest N. Wolff
Shandaa: In My Lifetime *by* Belle Herbert
Above the Arctic Circle *by* James A. Carroll
Reading the River *by* John Hildebrand
Sam O. White, Alaskan *by* Jim Rearden
Ten Thousand Miles with a Dog Sled *by* Hudson Stuck
Born on Snowshoes *by* Evelyn Berglund Shore
Kaiiroondak: Behind the Willows *by* Richard Martin
The Final Frontiersman *by* James Campbell
99 Days on the Yukon *by* Thomas McGuire
Trapline Chatter *by* Nancy Becker
Balancing Acts *by* Edward Hoagland

Printed in Great Britain
by Amazon